ALICE HART-DAVIS & MOLLY HINDHAUGH

Be BEAUTIFUL

EVERY GIRL'S GUIDE TO HAIR, SKIN & MAKE-UP

Contents

Molly

Everyone wants to look their best. But how do you work out how to do it? Ask your friends? Flip through magazines? Surf the internet? All these can give you different ideas, but it can get very confusing. I found I had so many questions about how to look after my skin and how to use make-up that I hardly knew where to begin.

So I asked Mum. What's the best way to keep your face clean (and spot-free!)? What can you do with eyeliner to make it look a bit different? What are the things that you ought to do (and how often do you really need to do them?) and what can you try when you want to do something fun?

Alice

When Molly started asking me about everything from moisturizers to mascara, it wasn't too hard to give her answers. I'm a health and beauty journalist and, over the years, my job has given me a good idea of what works best.

Over time, one question led to another, ranging from how to deal with spots to how to style your hair, via how to choose the right things to eat. When I wrote everything down, this book began to emerge.

What it's about is getting to grips with the basics of skin care, discovering the fun of make-up and learning how to look your best, and doing it all in a way that isn't going to cost the earth – in terms of both money and resources.

We hope, whatever your questions, that you find the answers – and more – in here.

HAIR

I want hair that looks great without my having to spend too much time on it. Blow-drying, straightening, crimping, teasing ... it's all too much bother. But I want to know how to do them for special occasions.

Hair

I know there's a style out there that suits me – but how to find it? And which of the zillion and one hair-care products will work best?

Keeping it clean

It's not just a case of slapping on the shampoo.

Q How often should I wash my hair? Can I do it every day?
As often as you want. Lots of hair experts say it does your hair no harm to wash it every day.

Q But what about stripping out all the natural oils?
Ah yes. There's another bunch of hair experts who say that it is much better to wash hair as little as possible.

Q But not washing your hair at all is disgusting! Won't it look gross?
The idea is that you rinse your hair to wash away sweat and dirt, but without shampoo. After six weeks, if you can tough it out that long, it settles down and yes, it does usually look a bit ... sleeker than usual, but nice and shiny as the natural oils make your hair glossy.

Q So which is right?
Decide what's best for you and go with it; there's no right or wrong.

Q If my hair looks awful in the morning and I haven't got time to wash it, what can I do?
Invest in some dry shampoo (yes, really), a kind of powder that you spray through your hair and rub into the roots so that it absorbs some of the excess oil; then brush it out and your hair should look better. If you don't have dry shampoo, you can try baby powder, but it's clumpier so harder to use without turning your scalp white and floury-looking.

Q Sometimes when I've washed my hair it feels all lank and sticky when I'm drying it.
You probably haven't rinsed it properly. Give it another few seconds under the shower, just to make sure.

Q What does conditioner actually do?
It smooths down the cuticle (the outside surface of the hair) so that it lies flat. That means it feels smoother and is much easier to comb or brush through after washing.

Tip
If you're having a bad hair day, try slicking it back in a tight ponytail or under a hairband. If it's going greasy, add some gel, so the wet-look effect seems deliberate. Or wear a hat!

Q What if you use too much conditioner? I've read that you should avoid over-conditioning your hair.

You can't really over-condition hair. Each strand of hair is a bit like a sponge; it will absorb what it needs and the rest washes off. If your hair feels sticky after you've used conditioner, then it might be the wrong sort for your hair, or maybe you could have rinsed it out a bit more thoroughly.

How to wash your *hair properly*

1 Wet your hair really thoroughly. Get a 50p-sized blob of shampoo in the palm of your hand (use more if your hair is long or thick). Rub your hands together so that you get the shampoo all over them, over each finger and the backs of your hands, too.

2 Start working your soapy fingers into the roots of your hair. If you start on the crown of your head, don't forget to take your hands up the back of your head and to do the bits round behind your ears. Before you reach for the shampoo again, put more water on your hair. This helps to spread the shampoo better across your scalp.

3 Massage the shampoo into the roots. You don't need to lather up the rest of your hair; the roots are what gets dirty and just rinsing the shampoo through will get the rest clean.

4 Then rinse, very thoroughly. If your hair is really dirty, shampoo a second time.

5 Smooth conditioner over the ends of your hair (you don't need it on the scalp).

6 Rinse really well.

Shampoo & conditioner

Work out which products will make a real difference to how your hair looks and feels.

Q **There are so many shampoos to choose from! How do I know which one is right for me?**
First, decide what kind of hair you've got (thick/coarse, fine/flyaway, greasy/oily, dry/brittle). There are shampoos promising to do everything from moisturizing your hair to giving it more volume, in every supermarket and chemist. They will all get your hair clean. What you want is something that leaves your hair feeling nice, too. The bad news is that you may have to try lots of different ones; the good news is that it won't necessarily be the most expensive one that works best.

Q **What kind of hair do I have?**
Greasy hair looks as if it needs a wash every morning. Greasy hair is normal in your teens when your hormones send your oil-producing glands into overdrive.
Dry hair feels rough or brittle and dry.
Fine hair baby-soft, thin hair without much volume.

Frizzy hair fuzzes up into hard-to-control curls and frizz if you don't dry it smooth.
Normal hair looks greasy when it's dirty; may get dry at the ends.

Q **What if it's greasy on the scalp and dry at the ends?**
Wash it with a gentle shampoo, and condition the ends to keep them soft.

Q **Do I need to change my shampoo every now and again so my hair doesn't get too used to it?**
No. That's an old wives' tale.

Q **If I use styling products, do I need a special detox shampoo to get rid of them?**
Unless you are using buckets of styling

Cheap shampoo or posh shampoo?

Avoid dirt-cheap shampoo. It's not that different from washing-up liquid. It will clean your hair but leave it feeling like straw. Try using a mid-priced product from a famous-name hairdresser. These contain plenty of high-tech ingredients and do a brilliant job. The really expensive ones have fabulously complex formulae designed to help fragile, over-processed, chemically treated hair. Your hair shouldn't need that sort of help.

Make your own conditioning treatments

Scalp-soother

Soothe and moisturize your scalp with one of the following: coconut oil, olive oil, almond oil or special hair oil. Massage the oil carefully all over your scalp, then wrap your hair in a towel for at least 10 minutes. Ideally, leave it on overnight – wrap your pillow in another towel – and wash it out in the morning.

Avocado conditioner

Pick a very ripe, soft avocado, so that you can mash it really smooth. If it seems too thick, dilute it with a little olive oil or coconut milk before you start. If it's not really smooth, it makes it difficult to rinse all the green gunk out of your hair and you'll find yourself picking bits out for days. Massage into your hair and leave for 10 minutes before rinsing out.

Pre-shampoo booster

Whisk up a couple of eggs and massage them into your hair. Yes, it feels revolting, all slimy and gloopy, but it will leave your hair shiny once you have washed it out. Make sure you use cool water. If it's hot, there's a danger that the eggs will scramble. Massage into your hair and leave for 10 minutes before rinsing out.

products like sticky moulding wax, you shouldn't need a special kind of shampoo to get your hair clean.

Q Can you use mayonnaise as conditioner?

You could – but because of all the egg yolks and oils in it, it might work better as a pre-shampoo conditioning treatment (rub it in, leave it for 15 minutes, then wash it out). This way it smells less bad too.

Hair hazards

Eek! How do I avoid them?

Split ends

Q How do I know if I've got split ends? Can I fix them?

Look closely at the very ends of your hair. If each hair is divided into two, like a little fish-tail, you have split ends. They're a sign of wear, caused by things like over-styling with heated tongs, or too much brushing. You can't mend them – you need to get them trimmed off.

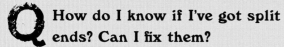

split ends

Dandruff

Q Ugh, where does it come from and why?

It's a scalp condition caused by a yeast-like micro-organism called pityrosporum ovale. Everyone has it on their scalp but in some people it gets out of control and makes lots of flakes of dead scalp skin fall out of your hair.

Q And how do you get rid of it?

Because it's caused by a naturally occurring thing, you can't actually get rid of dandruff for good. You have to settle for controlling it with anti-dandruff shampoos.

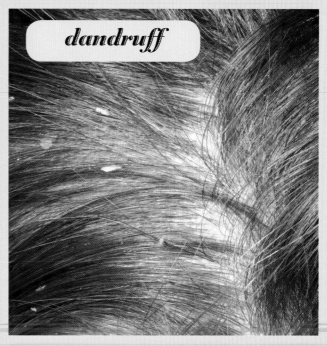

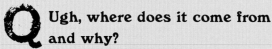

dandruff

Q What if anti-dandruff shampoos don't work?

Then the problem might be some other scalp condition like psoriasis or eczema. If you think it might be one of these, go and see your doctor.

Swimming

Q What does swimming-pool water do to your hair?

The chlorine in pool water acts like bleach: it lifts pigment from the hair and roughs up the cuticle, making hair look dull. Once the cuticle is damaged, other chemicals can get into the hair and make it more brittle.

Q How can I stop it?

Wet your hair through with normal, unchlorinated water before you get into the pool. That way, your hair is too full of normal water to soak up much chlorine. Wash your hair immediately after swimming, preferably with a special anti-chlorine shampoo, and use lots of conditioner.

Q Can pool water really make blonde hair go green?

Yes. It's not the chlorine that does it, but copper sulphate, a blue mineral salt which is put in pools to kill algae. It gets in through the damaged cuticle of the hair. Blue salts plus pale yellow hair equals a green tint.

Which hairbrush?

PADDLE BRUSH
USE FOR smoothing out long hair; blow-drying hair smooth.

VENT BRUSH
USE FOR detangling thick, wavy or curly hair; blow-drying thick hair.

ROUND BRUSH
USE FOR blow-drying hair, either to make curls, or to keep tension on the hair while drying it smooth.

WOODEN HAIR BRUSH
USE FOR hair that tends to go static – the wood discourages the build-up of static.

NATURAL-BRISTLE BRUSHES
USE FOR smoothing out hair – the rubber pad is good for discouraging static and the natural bristles will spread the hair's natural oils through the hair.

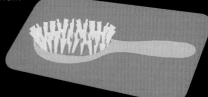

Hair colour

Would it brighten up your hair – or would it be a major mistake?

Q **I SO want to dye my hair! What colour will look best?**

The sensible answer:

You want a colour not too far removed from what you started with. If it's for an all-over colour, it's best to go only a shade or two darker or lighter, or it may clash with your skin tone.

The "who cares?" answer:

Teenagers don't have to be "sensible" with hair colour (well, depending on what view your parents and teachers take), so you can experiment. You can get away with all sorts of colours that would look just dreadful on an older face and against an older skin.

Think first!

How you wear your hair, and its colour, make a huge statement about who you are and what you're trying to say to the world, and a stand-out colour is a quick way to get a lot of attention. You might like that (if your friends say it's cool and looks good); you might not (if other people stare, tease or, worse, mock you for it). It's just something to think about before you reach for, say, permanent green...

Q **Which hair colour?**

If your skin is pink in tone, you'll look better with cool colours such as ashy blondes (rather than gold or yellow blondes) or dark brown.

If your skin is very pale and creamy, you can get away with any colour, even red.

If your skin is sallow with yellow undertones, warm strong colours will look good – golden blondes, or rich browns.

If your skin is olive, it will look perfect with very dark brown or black hair.

Q **What do I use?**

Semi-permanent colour will last for about six weeks; permanent dye will be with you for good, but because your hair keeps growing, you'll need to keep colouring the roots every 8 – 12 weeks, depending on how fast your hair grows.

Q **How hard is it to get brown hair to go blonde?**

It's tricky, because it's not a one-step process, and it depends on how brown your hair is to start with (mousy is much easier to convert than brunette). First, you need to use a pre-lightener product, which takes the normal colour out of your hair, before you start with the blonde dye. And how well the first step works has a big impact on how well the blonde dye will work.

What colour should I go?

start col \ finish col	white-blonde	blonde	red	brunette	black
blonde	Quite easy. Results depend on how blonde you are to start with.	X	Easier for pale than dark blondes. Aim for strawberry blonde first.	Easy. You may need to tint your eyebrows to match.	Easy to do, tricky to live with. It's not so easy to reverse.
mousy	Not hard, but it's a hard colour to wear.	Quite easy and might suit you really well.	Not hard; try a gentle red that warms up your natural colour.	Should be easy and could look great.	Easy, but black won't look natural on you.
red	Do it bit by bit before you opt for platinum.	Again, go gradually, in stages. May just go coppery.	X	Deepen your natural colour before you go dark brown.	Will look hard on your skin tone, particularly if you are Celtic-fair.
brunette	Needs lots of bleaching, may leave hair feeling "fried".	Do it slowly, with professional help (or risk going ginger).	Aim for auburn or chestnut, to enhance your natural colour.	X	Easy, but still a harsh colour to carry off.
black	Not recommended. May look very odd.	Stripping so much colour means the condition will suffer.	Why would you want to? Try red streaks for starters.	Tricky. Will need lots of intensive conditioning afterwards.	X

How to get *party hair*

YOU WILL NEED
An old swimming cap or a plastic bag
Non-permanent spray colour

1 Get an old swimming cap or a plastic bag and make holes all over it. Pull it on, then, using a wooden skewer or knitting needle, fish out bits of hair so that they stick out through the cap all over your head. If you want your highlights to be subtle, make the bits thin; if you want them more obvious, go for fat and chunky ones.

2 Spray the bits of hair with your colour. Let them dry before you remove the cap.

You could also try making small plaits or bunches in your hair and dipping the ends of these into hair colour.

Q What if I want my hair to look fun just for a party, not, like, for ever?

Then get some fun colours of spray-in, wash-out hair colour or hair gel, or hair "mascara", and see what you can do with them.

Bear in mind that the darker your hair is, the less the colours are likely to show up, unless you go for silver and gold.

Tip

Any hair colour will look better if the hair is in great condition. Try deep-conditioning treatments regularly to get your hair in good shape before you dye it, and afterwards, to make the most of the colour.

Q Are there any reasons I shouldn't use hair dye?

Three things:

1. It so often goes wrong, or just looks dreadful.

2. It's not uncommon to get allergic reactions.

3. Dark hair dyes in particular often contain a chemical called PPD (para-phenylenediamine), and research studies have appeared to show a connection between dark dyes and an increased risk of cancer.

Q Cancer? How can they sell the stuff?

It's not proved beyond doubt. There seems to be an adverse reaction in people who use these dyes more than nine times a year. But the studies certainly raise enough questions over dark hair dye to make it a worry.

Q What about peroxide – what will that do to my hair and is it dangerous?

It will gradually bleach the colour out of your hair, depending on how much you use at once. It's not dangerous, but it is just bleach and there are plenty of blonde dyes that don't contain bleach and are much kinder to your hair.

How to find a hairstyle that suits your face

First you need to work out what your face shape is. Pull your hair back off your face and either take a picture, head on to the camera, or look at your reflection in the mirror and, using an eyeliner pencil or a lipstick, draw the outline of your face on the mirror, then step back and see what sort of shape it makes.

A heart-shaped face

GO FOR a shape that will balance out the way your face gets narrower at the jaw. Anything chin-length, like a long bob will work. Long hair looks good swept back off your face to show off your cheekbones. AVOID styles that make the wide part of your head look wider.

An oval face

GO FOR whatever you like – lucky you, you can get away with almost anything from super-short to long, particularly with styles that sweep the hair back off your face.

A rectangular face

GO FOR a style that makes your face appear shorter and breaks up the strong lines which can make your face look a bit hard. That could mean a fringe, layers that add fullness at the top of your head, layers to make wispy bits around your cheeks, or really short styles – particularly if you have thick or curly hair, as this will give instant volume.
AVOID long droopy styles that fall straight down past your cheeks – these will just make a long face look longer.

A round face

GO FOR anything that takes the emphasis away from the wide, middle point of your face, particularly if your hair is curly or wavy. You could try layers to add volume on top, or a style that comes straight down below your chin and then flicks out, or a side parting, so that you can sweep one side of your hair behind your ear.
AVOID any round-looking hairstyles, such as a short chunky bob, or a round chin-length style; these will only make your face look fatter. Also avoid centre partings; they tend to emphasize the width of your face.

A square face

GO FOR softer, more "girlie" styles with waves or layers or bits that fall in round the face, to help break up the square shape. A choppy fringe will help, too. And if your hair is fine, a long, straight style will be flattering to a wide jaw.
AVOID any tough-looking geometric cuts or square-cut fringes. They will only make your face look squarer, as will anything shorter than chin-length.

Tips

✱ Try on some wigs and hairpieces. Department stores have lots to play with.

✱ Find a website with a try-this-hairstyle-for-size option where you can import your own photo, then drop a number of styles onto it to see how you look.

Hairdressers

Having your hair cut can be nerve-racking but, before they start cutting, a good hairdresser will always talk you through exactly what they're planning to do and what it will look like. Don't be afraid to ask lots of questions. It's your hair, you are the one who's paying, and they'll want you to be happy with the result.

Q How do I get a hairdresser to cut my hair how I want it?

Be as clear as you can about how you'd like your hair to look.

✳ If you have a picture of the style you want, take it along and discuss it with the stylist, rather than just showing it to them.

✳ If you want a fringe, say how long it should be and whether you'd like it wispy or cut in a solid line.

✳ Point out if you usually have your parting in a particular place, and if you need to be able to tie your hair back for any reason.

✳ Give your hairdresser as much information as you can.

Expert tips

From Susan Baldwin, UK creative director and head of colour for John Frieda:

✳ Your teens are a great time to experiment with your hair colour. You can get away with anything just because you're young, so if you want to try things out, go for it. You don't have to play safe.

✳ Hair dye won't always go the colour on the packet when it's on your hair. So don't expect miracles.

✳ If you're going to try something a bit extreme, you'll need to have short hair for it to look good. Get a great cut before you colour it. Bleaching takes its toll on hair, and if your hair is long, it will just get too brittle and start to break off.

✳ Get some expert advice – most salons are happy to offer you a free consultation with a colourist. Even if you don't take them up on what they suggest, you will get five minutes or so of their expertise and it will help you to decide what you want to do with your hair.

✳ Most of us look better with slightly lighter hair around our faces. So if you want just a few highlights or lowlights, try putting them at the front. And remember that less is more. You can always build up and add to the colour that you've got.

✳ Any kind of extreme colour, whether it's ultra-blonde, hard black or bright ginger, is quite hard on your skin; even if you are young and lovely, a bright hair colour may make you look a bit pale and ill. So bear in mind that you'll need to wear some make-up to stop yourself looking washed out!

Q And what if it's a disaster?
You can throw a complete hissy fit, sob loudly, or sulk. Or – and we've all had to do this at some point – you can be brave and try to make the best of it. It's very difficult to laugh off a bad haircut, but it's one of life's learning processes – and you know what? Your hair will grow. But give that salon or stylist a miss the next time you're looking for a new cut.

What hairdressers say (and what they mean)

We're going to...

CHOP UP THE FRINGE A BIT
Cut vertically into the fringe so that it's not one solid line. Usually flattering.

USE GRADUATED LAYERS
Cut layers of different, overlapping, lengths into the hair.

RAZOR THE ENDS
Literally, cut the ends with a razor (which can tweak a bit), to give a slightly uneven finish.

GIVE IT A BIT MORE OOMPH Do something to boost the volume or the general impact that the cut makes.

GIVE YOU A BLUNT CUT
Cut the hair so that it's all one solid length.

USE A BIT OF PRODUCT
Use styling products to get the desired results. Ask if you'll need to buy the products if you want to copy the look.

MAKE IT CHOPPY
End up with more of a rough, chunky finish.

LAYER IT THROUGH THE MID-LENGTHS
Cut layers into longer hair, but starting half-way down the head.

DO SOMETHING RADICAL
Ask what they mean and how "radical" before you let them get started.

Hair-styling made easy

Practice makes perfect – so get practising!

Q **How do I get my hair to look smooth and shiny?**

You can use all the conditioners and smoothing potions that you like; the real secret to great-looking hair is in the blow-drying and styling. None of the models in magazines with the fabulous hair actually looks like that first thing in the morning.

Q **Are straighteners bad for your hair?**

Not if you...

✱ Use a heat-protecting spray on your hair first.

✱ Make sure hair is dry before you start.

✱ Don't use them too often.

Q **Why does it have to be dry? Some styling tips say hair should be "towel dry".**

The plates of the straightener are so hot that they will literally boil any water left in the hair. When water inside a strand of hair boils, it expands, damaging the hair and leaving it more fragile.

Smooth hair

1 Rough-dry hair so that it's three quarters dry. Separate out one section on the top of your head, then divide the rest of your hair into three or four sections.

2 Dry each section using a round brush with bristles all the way around the edge, or a paddle brush, which you hold at a right angle to the hair.

3 Start at the roots of the hair and move the dryer, and the brush, from the roots down to the tips of the hair ... again and again, until that section is dry. It takes a while, but it gets the cuticle properly smoothed down. Repeat with each section.

Pretty wavy hair

1 Start with hair 90 per cent dry. Comb a large blob of styling mousse evenly through your hair (if your hair is very dry and you want more of a moisturizing effect, you can mix a bit of body lotion in with the mousse).

2 Separate your hair into small sections. Twist each one round your finger until it is twisted up like a rope, then make it into a little loop and pin it against your head. Leave it to dry.

3 When you take the pins out, shake your head gently and the curls will fall into pretty waves. If you want to fluff the hair out a bit, turn your head upside-down and gently run your hands through the curls. Don't pull at them or brush them, because they'll flatten out and vanish.

Crimping

1 Make sure your hair is 100 per cent dry before you start, and apply a heat-protection product.

2 Crimp your hair in sections. Start at the back, doing the underneath layers first. Clamp the crimping irons onto the hair nearest to your head and work downwards. When you've finished the back section, work towards the front. It will probably take you quite a while.

You could also try crimping just a few sections of hair, as a contrast to the rest.

HAIR

How to straighten curly hair

1 Wash and condition hair, then comb through a smoothing or straightening balm.

2 Separate hair into sections and blow-dry them one by one, using a square paddle brush to help pull the hair smooth. Start with the blow-dryer at the roots and direct the hot air from the roots down to the tips while holding the hair taut.

3 If this doesn't get your hair straight enough, use straightening irons. Make sure your hair is dry first, and work in sections, smoothing the irons from roots to tips.

How to get smooth, frizz-free curls

1 After washing, towel-dry your hair, then apply leave-in conditioner or anti-frizz or curl-enhancing serum (if your hair is long and thick, use plenty). Comb it through with your fingers, then with a wide-toothed comb so that the product is spread through the hair. Let your hair dry naturally, or use a diffuser on the end of a hairdryer on a gentle setting. Don't brush the curls out as they form, or the hair will go into one great frizzy mass.

Q What can I do to stop my hair picking up static?

✽ Use a heat-protecting spray before blow-drying (most static gets in there during drying).

✽ Try using a natural-bristle brush which is less likely to generate static than a brush with plastic "bristles".

✽ Try "ionic" brushes with a ceramic barrel; they produce less static.

✽ Get a fabric-conditioning sheet (the sort that goes in the tumble-dryer) and run it over your hair. Sounds odd, but it works a treat.

Q How do volumizing hair products work?

They have ingredients that either coat each hair and bulk it out, or make the hairs stand away from each other. Either way, they make it look as if you've got more hair.

Q If I don't want to cover my hair in chemicals, are there natural styling products that work as well?

Not that work in the same way, but plenty of people use lemon juice, diluted with water, as a hair-texturizing spray and a hair-setting lotion. It's light, but a bit sticky, and if you're blonde it will give a bit of a bleaching effect.

Q What's the difference between normal shampoos and "natural"/organic shampoos?

Natural and organic shampoos contain more natural and organic ingredients, and usually don't contain sodium lauryl sulphate (SLS) (which is known to be irritating to the skin and can also make skin more sensitive) or paraben-based preservatives.

Q How organic is organic shampoo?

Read the bottle to find out. Companies can put the word "organic" on a bottle even if it contains only a drop of organic tea-tree oil. Any product certified by the Soil Association or EcoCert will contain almost nothing but organic ingredients.

3 WAYS TO BE GREENER IN YOUR HAIR CARE

✽ Don't wash your hair every day.

✽ Look for products with a high proportion of natural ingredients.

✽ If you're colouring your hair, look for dyes based on natural or vegetable colourings.

My face is always on show, so I feel a whole lot more confident if I have clear, healthy skin.

Face care

Skin develops a life of its own once you get into your teens – I never know what mine is going to do next. Everyone has a different piece of advice to offer. Cleanse like this... Exfoliate like that... Which is right for me? And what IS toner for, anyway?

Suss out your skin type

Before you worry about what to use on your skin, you need to work out what kind of skin you have.

 What's the secret of great skin?

* Keep it clean
* Keep it soft and supple
* Exfoliate regularly
* Keep it protected from the sun

It's that simple! But how you choose to clean your skin, and the products you use on it, will depend on the kind of skin you have.

DID YOU KNOW?

SOME SKIN-CARE EXPERTS HAVE ESTIMATED THAT 70 PER CENT OF US HAVE COMBINATION SKIN, SO REALLY THAT IS WHAT OUGHT TO BE CLASSED AS "NORMAL".

Different skin types

Dry
Often feels dry, tight and a bit rough, especially after washing

Oily
Looks greasy, with enlarged pores around the nose and chin, and gets more than its fair share of spots and blackheads

Normal
Lovely clear, smooth-textured skin that is neither oily nor dry

Combination
Dry on cheeks, oily in the T-zone (across the forehead and down the centre of your face)

Take the tissue test

To work out which skin type you have, try this:

1. Wash and dry your face, then wait for half an hour.

2. Take a few pieces of fine tissue paper and press them onto your cheeks, nose, chin and forehead.

RESULT:

✱ If the paper sticks and picks up oily patches from your skin, then you have oily skin.

✱ If it doesn't stick anywhere, your skin is normal or dry (if it feels tight after you've washed it, it's dry).

✱ If it sticks on your forehead, nose and chin, you have combination skin.

FACE CARE

Keeping it clean

Good skin care starts with proper cleansing.

Q **So how SHOULD I clean my face?**

Massage some light cleansing lotion into your face and neck and work it well into the skin. Then wipe it off with a flannel or muslin cloth that you've dipped in a basin of warm water and wrung out. It feels good and your skin will be left clean and soft, rather than dried out. This should get off any make-up, as well as general grime left on your skin at the end of the day.

Q **Won't the flannel get filthy?**

Yes, it will, so invest in a few of them (or cut up an old towel into flannel-sized pieces) and chuck them in the washing machine (on a hot wash) after you've used them a couple of times, to keep them free from bacteria. What's good about flannels is that they're endlessly re-usable, so you won't

You don't need a special face wash

Any of the following can be used to clean your face. Massage into your skin, then wipe off with a hot, damp flannel.

* Almond oil or sunflower oil
* Baby lotion
* A thicker cream cleanser

* Cleansing balms (a bit sticky, but great for removing eye make-up)
* Oil-based cleanser
* Any moisturizing lotion

be cluttering up landfill rubbish sites with disposable wipes and clods of cotton wool.

Q Do I really have to do this morning and night? If I've done it thoroughly at night, my skin won't be dirty again by morning, will it?

No, fair enough. It's more important to get your face clean before you go to bed. In the mornings, you can get away with a quick splash of water to freshen up your skin and wake you up.

Q What exactly is toner and do I need to use it?

Toner is a special runny liquid that you can use to help remove the last traces of cleanser from the skin, or as a quick skin-freshener. It's optional rather than vital. And if you've already used a damp cloth around your face, there's not much more that toner can do.

What not to use

Choose what you use with care.

Q **Can't I just use face wipes?**
Not unless you have no alternative. Yes, they will do a good job of removing make-up, mascara, eyeliner and general dirt. But if the cleansing fluid they are soaked in is strong enough to get all that off your face, it's not something that should then be left ON your face. If you do use them, splash your face with water afterwards, or wipe it with a damp cloth. Face wipes aren't very eco-friendly, either, since you use them once and then chuck them away.

Q **Shouldn't I use an anti-bacterial face wash to keep my face really clean and make sure I don't get spots?**
Not unless spots are a real problem. Yes, it will leave your skin feeling squeaky clean, but that is because these products strip all the natural protective oils from your skin, which may well end up feeling uncomfortably tight and dry. Then it might react by going into oil-producing overdrive and pump out even more oil to try to rebalance itself. If you're plagued by spots and you have tried all the gentle, natural ways to keep them under control, then you might need an anti-bacterial wash to keep the oiliness of skin in check.

Q **What about soap and water?**
No: using soap and water also strips the skin of oil and you end up with dehydrated, oily skin, which is even worse.

Q **How can skin be dehydrated if it's oily?**
Skin needs water to keep it moist and oil (just a bit) to keep it soft and supple and the two things are quite different.

Q **But I've heard people say you can clean your face with oil. Doesn't that just give you more spots?**
Oddly enough, it doesn't, though it depends on what sort of oil you use. Face-cleansing oils are usually light and runny and not that different, in terms of their chemical structure, from sebum, the oil that your face produces. This means that as well as being really good for dissolving grime and make-up, the cleansing oil will also bind with and lift away any excess oils on your skin, so it's good for people with oily skin.

> ## DID YOU KNOW?
> IN ONE SQUARE CENTIMETRE OF SKIN, YOU HAVE 250 SWEAT GLANDS AND 400 NERVE ENDINGS.

Exfoliating

Clean away the dead cells and let your skin glow.

Q What is exfoliating?

Exfoliating is scuffing off the outermost skin cells. It sounds a bit gruesome, but it's not, because your skin is made up of many layers of cells and the ones in the very top layer are dead anyway, though they stick around on the surface until they flake off or are polished off.

Q Why do I need to exfoliate?

The dead skin cells are too small to see, but if lots of them stick together they can make your skin look dull and greyish. When you exfoliate, you remove them and as a result your skin looks brighter and fresher.

Q So how do I do it?

You could get a special facial scrub and use it GENTLY, but many facial scrubs are quite scratchy and if you rub your face hard with them, your skin can get sore and irritated. But you don't need to use a scrub. If you cleanse your face with a flannel or muslin cloth that has been wrung out in hot water every day, that will be enough to keep your skin exfoliated.

Q And the old surface...?

This has rubbed away, on your clothing, your sheets, in the shower ... and you haven't even noticed it go. Gentle exfoliating is just helping this along.

Q Won't exfoliating just wear my skin away?

No, because new skin cells are being made the whole time. They start deep down in the skin and work their way up to the surface, which takes about a month.

Q What if my skin is dry? Should I exfoliate less?

No, exfoliating is good for dry skin. It might sound more logical to leave dry skin alone, but removing dead cells helps improve its texture and allows your moisturizer to get straight into the skin cells where it's needed.

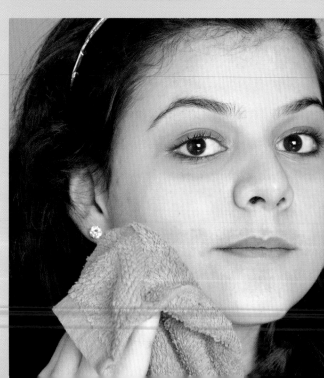

The secret of soft, supple skin

Sometimes skin needs help to stay in top condition.

Q **Do I need to use moisturizer?**
Not unless your skin feels a bit tight and dry after cleansing. If it does, use moisturizer once your skin is clean, morning and evening. Pick one that suits your skin type (see next page to help you choose).

Q **When I put water on my face, doesn't that give the skin moisture?**
It does, but it lasts only until your skin dries out. Moisturizer helps trap water in the top layers of the skin to keep it soft, stopping skin from losing moisture.

DID YOU KNOW?
AN ADULT HUMAN SHEDS ABOUT 10 GRAMS OF DEAD SKIN CELLS EVERY DAY. GIVEN HOW LITTLE EACH CELL WEIGHS, THAT'S QUITE A LOT!

Why you need to keep your skin moisturized

Healthy skin cells are full and plump. They fit together snugly like bricks in a well-made wall, held together by natural skin oils called lipids, to form a barrier to the outside world. If the skin is in good condition, this barrier keeps moisture in and dirt and bacteria out.

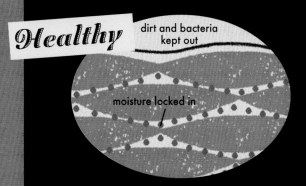

Healthy

dirt and bacteria kept out

moisture locked in

BUT if the skin becomes dry, the barrier doesn't work as it should. Water escapes from the cells and evaporates, leaving the skin cells more shrivelled, with gaps between them, and dirt and bacteria can find their way in.

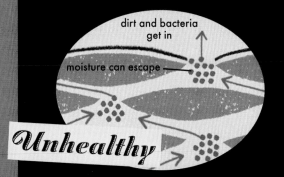

dirt and bacteria get in

moisture can escape

Unhealthy

FACE CARE

Q Do I need an anti-ageing moisturizer? Will that stop me from ever getting wrinkles?
No! Don't even think of using any of the heavy-duty or high-tech anti-ageing creams. Those are aimed at women who are 30-plus. They're expensive and designed to prop up skin that is beginning to suffer from the effects of time. You just don't need them.

Q So what's best for me?
Something simple, and preferably natural, to keep your skin healthy – and the good news is that this sort of skin care, unlike all those anti-ageing potions, needn't be expensive.

DID YOU KNOW?
BAMBAKOMALLOPHOBIA IS THE PHOBIA OF COTTON WOOL!

What sort of moisturizer should I use?

SKIN TYPE	MOISTURIZER
oily	You probably won't need a moisturizer at all, but if you do, pick a light gel or an oil-free lotion that will provide enough moisture without grease.
dry	If your skin is really dry, you might need a thicker, creamier moisturizer, but don't go for anything too heavy that could overload your skin or block pores.
normal	You may not need a moisturizer, but if you do, a lotion or light cream will work best.
combination	For combination skin, a lotion or gel-cream moisturizer is best.

How to give yourself a face massage

Give yourself a treat whenever you have the time. It's great for the skin (it boosts circulation in the tiny blood cells beneath the skin, so it makes skin glow) and helps prevent puffiness in the face. It releases tension in the muscles in the face that can make you look cross. It doesn't cost anything and you can do it with cleanser, moisturizer, face oil or olive oil.

1 Start at your collar bone and work upwards, sweeping your hands up your neck to your chin, from the point of your chin out towards your ears, and up across your cheeks to your forehead. Use firm upward strokes. You're using the right amount of pressure if you can feel your fingers working on the muscles beneath the surface of the skin. Don't press too hard – you don't want to drag the skin about.

2 To relieve tension around the eyes – a great one when you've been studying hard and your forehead feels all crumpled with concentration – press your ring fingers onto the inner corners of your eyebrows. Then sweep each of those fingers in a circular movement out around the line of the eyebrow, down around the lower bit of the eye socket, and back up to where you started. Do this 10 times.

3 Starting at your chin, use gentle pinching movements and work upwards, along the edge of your jaw and up the side of your face, to your temples. With your fingers folded over into a loose fist, rotate your knuckles gently across your face, starting at the chin.

Home-made skin care

You can be green and save money – make your own.

Cucumber-juice toner

Mild and softening cucumber is good for any kind of skin.

1. Juice a cucumber, then strain the juice through a sieve to get rid of any pulpy bits.

2. Wipe the juice over your face after cleansing. Store in the fridge for up to three days.

Home-made face scrub

Exfoliate the natural way with kitchen-cupboard basics.

1. Grind up a handful of porridge oats in a blender. Add a teaspoonful of caster sugar.

2. Take a small amount of this powdery mix in your hand and add enough water to work it into a paste.

3. Rub the mix gently over your face, concentrating on the chin and nose and avoiding the delicate skin around your eyes.

4. Rinse with warm water.

You can also make a gentle scrub by mixing a dessertspoonful of sugar into a handful of your normal cleanser. Use as above.

Banana face mask

Banana is soothing for dry skin.

1. Mash together half a ripe banana,

a tablespoonful of honey and a tablespoonful of thick cream.

2. Smooth over the face and leave for at least 15 minutes, then wash off.

3. Store the extra in the fridge. Use within three days.

Strawberry face mask

The malic acid in strawberries helps to brighten and tone oily skin.

1. Mash up three large ripe strawberries. You can also add a teaspoonful of honey to make the mixture less slippery and more sticky if you like.

2. Smooth onto your skin – but don't leave it on too long because strawberries are quite acidic (try three minutes the first time), then rinse off.

Avocado face mask

The oils in avocados make them rich and moisturizing on the skin.

1. Mash half an avocado until it is as smooth as you can get it. Make sure you choose a ripe one, otherwise it just won't mash however hard you try.

2. Massage the mash onto your face and leave it for 15 minutes, then rinse off. Don't panic when it starts to go brown: it does that when oxygen gets to it.

strawberry

avocado

banana

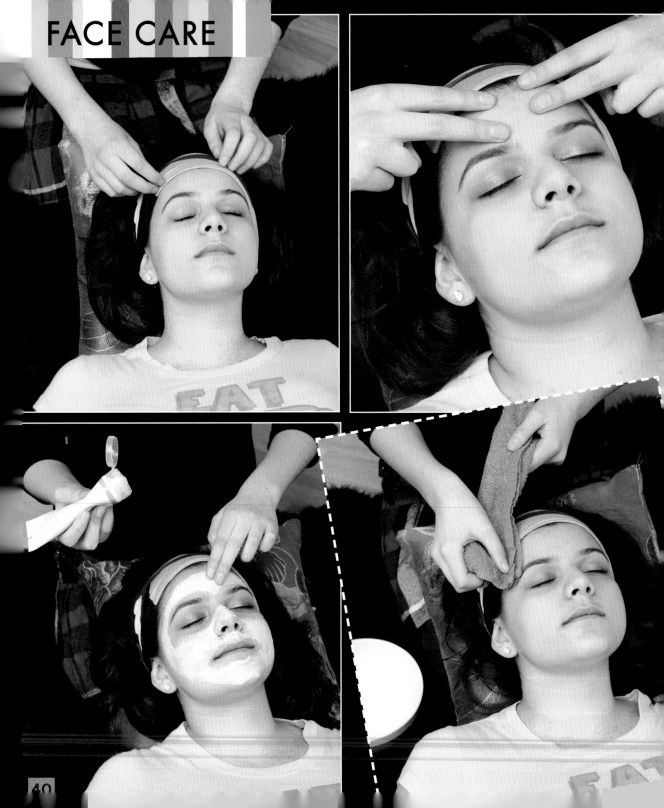

How to do a mini facial

YOU WILL NEED
A friend!
A hairband
Cleansing lotion
A clean face flannel
A bowl of hot water
A face mask
Moisturizer

1 Get your friend to put on a hairband to push the hair off her face. Then pile some cushions on the floor so she can lie down on her back and you can sit behind her head.

2 Start by massaging a gentle cleansing lotion into her face. Starting at the point of the chin, make little circular movements, working outwards to the edge of the jaw, then up across the face.

3 Do sweeping movements, using the flats of your hands and your middle fingers, up from the point of the chin to the temples.

4 Make scissors with your first two fingers of each hand and put them, slightly interlaced, on the middle of your friend's forehead, then pull each hand out to the side of the face. Repeat five times.

5 Massage gently around the eyes. Put your index (first) fingers on the point near the nose where the eyebrows start, then sweep them gently out around the eyebrows, down around the outside of the eyes and the top of the cheeks, and back to where you started. Do this five times, and each time you reach the starting-point, press it gently (it's an acupressure point, so this can help people feel more relaxed).

6 Squeeze the flannel out in the hot water, then use it to wipe off the cleansing lotion.

7 Carefully apply the face mask, avoiding the eye area (the skin here is more delicate, so it's best to leave it be). Wait five minutes.

8 Wipe off the mask, using the damp flannel, until all traces of the mask have gone.

9 Gently massage a little light moisturizer into your friend's face. You could use the same massage movements as before.

Tip

Even if you feel you don't know what you're doing, do all the movements slowly and confidently as if you were an expert. Your friend will be amazed!

Sensitive skin, eczema & skin allergies

Itchy, scaly skin can make life miserable, so you need ways to get it under control.

Q **What's the best way to cure eczema?**

Unfortunately you can't cure it. It's something that you need to learn to "manage", so that you avoid doing things that make it flare up. Eczema makes skin very dry, so treatment means keeping skin as well moisturized as possible, using a product that doesn't irritate it, and if it does get red and sore and itchy, using a corticosteroid cream, which helps reduce the redness and inflammation. The natural alternative to this is phytosterol creams, which are made with a soya-bean extract that aims to decrease inflammation in the same way.

Q **What makes eczema flare up?**

It depends on the kind of eczema you have, but it usually happens because you come into contact with something to which your skin is hyper-sensitive. That could be something that irritates it, or it could be something that causes an allergic reaction, which makes your skin go rashy and bumpy and sore. This can happen if you touch something you're allergic to, such as skin products with fragrance in them, or rubber.

eczema

Q How does stress make eczema worse?

Science has yet to prove how stress and eczema are linked – though anyone who has eczema will tell you that the two are closely related.

Q What are the main ingredients in cosmetics that can irritate the skin?

The worst culprits are fragrances, followed by sodium lauryl (and to a lesser extent sodium laureth) sulphate (the foaming ingredient in shampoo and bubble bath) and soap.

Q So if fragrances, soap and detergents are the worst things, can they make my skin more sensitive, too?

Yes.

Q Is there anything I can do to make my skin less sensitive?

You can try more natural products, or ones that don't contain sodium lauryl sulphate or fragrance (which is often listed as "parfum") and see if your skin reacts less to them.

Q Why are so many people allergic to cosmetics?

There are many ingredients in cosmetics that can provoke a reaction.

When people say they're allergic to cosmetics, they usually mean that these make their skin react, or that their skin is sensitive to them. Proper allergy is a bit different. That is when the body's immune system decides that something – whether it is grass pollen or nail varnish – is a dangerous threat and suddenly overreacts to it. The trouble with allergies like this is that they can take a long time to develop, as the body becomes "sensitized". That means you can use something like a face cream for years and then suddenly your body decides it is an allergen and when you use it you get a rash, or your eyes and nose start to itch and water, or your throat feels tight.

Q Are natural products less irritating?

Often, but not always.

Q Are "hypo-allergenic" and "dermatologically tested" products OK for sensitive skin or people who get eczema?

They're worth a try, but you need to bear in mind that all "hypo-allergenic" means is that something is less likely to cause an allergic reaction than other products, not that it definitely won't cause a reaction. "Dermatologically tested" just means that through being tested the product has reached a certain standard of safety or effectiveness.

Spots are a nightmare. They look disgusting, take AGES to go away and always turn up at the worst possible time, like when there's a party. Mum usually says, "What spot? Where?" and "Just ignore it – it'll go away." But it's pretty hard to act normally if you've got a huge glowing spot on your chin.

So what can you do to stop yourself getting spots? What's the best way to hide them? And how can you get them to vanish a.s.a.p?

What causes spots?

Nobody wants them, but most of us get them anyway. Is it what we eat, or how we live? Or are they just a fact of life?

Q Why, oh why do I have to get spots?

It's all thanks (or no thanks) to the level of testosterone, one of the sex hormones, in your body. Your hormone levels are all over the place as you go through puberty. If you are over-sensitive to testosterone, you're likely to have greasier skin, and to be plagued by spots.

Q Isn't testosterone a male hormone? Does that mean boys get worse spots?

Testosterone **is** a male hormone, but girls have it too – just less of it. It's how your body reacts to testosterone that decides whether you get spots. So no, boys don't have worse spots.

Q Where do spots come from?

During puberty, your body produces more of the sex hormones testosterone and oestrogen. If your body is sensitive to testosterone, your sebaceous glands – the thousands of tiny oil-producing glands in your skin – will start over-producing a greasy oil called sebum. At the same time, the testosterone makes the tiny cells that line the way into the oil glands thicker and stickier, so your pores are more likely to get clogged up. If this happens, the bacteria that normally live in your sebaceous glands start to break down the sebum and the glands can become inflamed. As the inflammation gets worse, you develop a red spot.

Q Why do I get more spots down the middle of my face and on my forehead than on my cheeks?

That T-zone of forehead, nose and chin has more oil-producing glands than the rest of your face, which is why it is more likely to get spotty.

Q Can other things cause spots?

If spots show up after you have eaten particular foods, such as shellfish, or strawberries, then you may be allergic to that food. If they tend to appear regularly, a few days before your period, they are certainly hormonal.

Tip

To help avoid spots, stop touching your face: it transfers bacteria and dirt from your fingertips to your skin.

If they only ever crop up before exams or other stressful "life events", then they are hormonal but provoked by stress.

Q Can you blame your parents?
Not entirely. The genes passed on to you by your parents are partly responsible for how your skin behaves. So if your mum or dad suffered from acne, you might, too. But then again, you might be lucky.

Q Does having a dirty face mean you get more spots?
Technically, no, since hormones are to blame, rather than dirt. But having said that, it is better and much more hygienic to have clean skin. If your face has become dirty, it has probably picked up plenty of bacteria, which won't help with spot prevention. And having a greasy fringe flopping onto your forehead can make spots worse too.

DID YOU KNOW?
TO A DERMATOLOGIST, ALL SPOTS ARE ACNE, WHETHER YOU'VE GOT ONE BLEMISH OR A HUNDRED.

Tip
Don't rub or pick at bumps where you think spots are forming. It will make them worse.

T-zone

Getting spots

The natural approach

If you prefer natural remedies and avoid harsher medications, try this regime suggested by the holistic therapists at Neal's Yard Remedies:

✱ Keep skin clean, to keep your pores free of sebum and grime.

✱ Don't use harsh exfoliating scrubs – they can stress your skin. A wrung-out flannel is enough.

✱ Learn face-massage techniques (see page 41) to prevent congestion under the skin, and so help to stop spots forming.

✱ Dab spots with a mixture of witch-hazel, tea-tree and palmarosa essential oils. Use one drop of each, mixed together; apply with a cotton bud.

✱ Steam your face once a week to help keep the pores clear.

✱ Learn some basic relaxation techniques. This may not seem remotely relevant to the spots on your face, but because stress makes spots worse, the two things ARE connected.

✱ Eat healthily – plenty of fresh fruit and vegetables, lean protein, nuts, seeds, oily fish and complex carbohydrates such as brown rice and wholemeal bread, and as little sugar and artificial additives as possible.

NATURAL ANTI-SPOT REMEDIES
Tea-tree oil and colloidal silver
These both tackle the bacteria that help to cause spots.

How to steam your face

1. Fill a bowl with hot (not boiling) water.
2. Add two drops of an aromatherapy oil such as soothing camomile, or lemongrass, which is good for oily skin.
3. Lean over the bowl and cover your head with a towel.
4. Stay like that for five minutes.
If you want, you can use a face mask after this stage – try one that has clay in it, which will help draw impurities out of the skin.
5. Afterwards, splash your face with cold water to close up the pores.

under control

The medical approach
No one should have to suffer with spots – and there are many ways your GP can help.

✳ Keep your face clean with a face wash designed for spotty skin, to de-grease the greasy bits and keep down levels of bacteria.

✳ Apply an anti-spot lotion twice a day after washing your face. Most such lotions contain a chemical called benzyl peroxide, which dries out spots and helps clear blackheads.

Try this routine for six weeks. If there is no improvement:

✳ Go and see your GP, who may prescribe an antibiotic cream, an anti-acne gel such as Isotrexin, or a course of antibiotics such as doxycycline. After six months, if there is still no improvement:

✳ Go back to your GP. They might suggest giving you a contraceptive pill called Dianette (don't panic, it does improve greasy skin), or they might refer you to a dermatologist. For severe acne that isn't responding to other treatment, your GP or your dermatologist might prescribe a drug called Roaccutane, which can work wonders on severe acne.

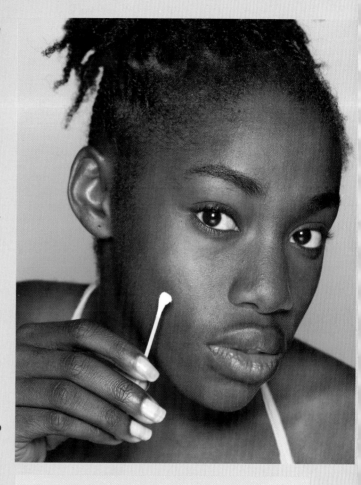

MEDICAL ANTI-SPOT REMEDIES
Benzyl peroxide
Found in normal anti-spot remedies in concentrations of between two and ten per cent. Dries out spots and helps clear blackheads.
Isotrexin gel
Available on prescription. Effective at controlling acne and calming inflammation.

Food, drink and spots

Q **Does it make a difference what I eat or drink?**

No. Even if you eat the greasiest, most fattening foods – burgers, fried breakfasts, chocolate – it doesn't have any effect on how greasy your skin will be.

Q **Is there anything I should avoid?**

Yes. Avoid drinking too much milk. One study of thousands of teenagers in the US showed those who drank more than half a litre of milk a day had far worse acne than those who didn't.

Q **If I drink loads of water, will that help "flush out" the spots?**

No. It sounds like a great idea, and it's much better for you to drink water than to drink fizzy drinks or tea or coffee or fruit juice, but it won't make any difference to whether you are spotty or not.

Q **But it's better for your skin, right? All the advice that you get in magazines says "Drink loads of water to help get rid of spots"!**

Drinking water is a healthy habit – every beautician I've ever met says it is the best beauty habit to get into – BUT there is no scientific evidence linking water-drinking to clearer skin.

Covering up

Luminous glowing spots? Here's how to make them vanish (well, almost).

Q Does wearing make-up to cover spots make them worse?

It can, if it clogs up the pores. If the make-up is powder-based and made from minerals, then it should be fine (powdery make-up helps soak up excess oil). Try not to smother your whole face in make-up. See if you can get by using a medicated blemish-cover stick.

Q What do blemish sticks actually do?

They contain antiseptic and anti-bacterial ingredients to help dry out spots and reduce inflammation. Tinted ones act like a concealer so help provide cover.

DID YOU KNOW?

If a celebrity grows a humungous spot before something vital like a live TV appearance, they speed-dial their dermatologist. One American dermatologist even has a 911 Pimple Emergency Service. This man injects the offending spot with a substance called triamcinolone (which, if you want to get technical, is an anti-inflammatory corticosteroid). This more or less melts the pimple away, but it costs an arm and a leg – over $100 per spot!

Two ways to cover up a spot

1 Use a blemish stick or concealer the same colour as your skin. Dab it on gently and if you need to, blend the colour with a fingertip. If it looks cakey or dry, use a bit of moisturizer to soften it into the skin. If it looks shiny, dust with face powder.

2 Using mineral-powder make-up and a special flat powder-brush, pat the powder gently onto the spot using the flat side of the brush until it has as good as vanished. Once it's done, DON'T TOUCH.

Prevention and cure

The basics, the latest science and the "miracle" remedies.

Q **Can't I just wash my face twice a day with soap and water? That's what the biology videos say we should do in order to avoid getting spots.**

Keeping your face clean is always a good idea, though soap isn't always the best thing to use as it tends to strip natural oils from the skin. There are plenty of face washes that will get rid of the dirt, oil and bacteria more gently. But this still won't alter whatever is going on with your hormones.

Q **But doesn't anti-bacterial face wash strip the skin and make it produce more oil?**

It's a question of finding a balance. You don't need strong face washes if your skin is normal, but if you get lots of spots, you need to do something to get the oiliness under control. Start with gentle cleansers or washes and if they don't do the trick, try stronger ones. The other part of the balancing act is that you need to do this without making your skin too dry. If using a face wash makes your cheeks dry, then moisturize them, but not the bits of your face that go greasy.

Q **How come people with dry skin still get spots?**

Because such people have oily patches, even if the rest of their skin is dry. What they need to do is moisturize the dry bits.

Q **What's "bacne"?**

A slangy term for having a spotty back.

Q **Could I get to see a dermatologist?**

You could, but it's not easy because there are relatively few dermatologists in the UK (450, compared with 10,000 in the USA). Most of them are tied up with hospital clinics dealing with people with really bad skin conditions.

But if you have bad skin it is still worth asking your GP to refer you to a dermatologist, because to dermatologists acne is not the end of the world, but a normal problem to which there are a variety of solutions.

Q Is it true you can get spots lasered off?

Not quite. There are several expensive high-tech systems that shine blue, or yellow, or red light onto the skin; this is supposed to help kill bacteria within the skin, to help clear up spots. One or two studies using these systems have shown good results, but this treatment doesn't always work as well as it is supposed to.

Q There are loads of amazing natural spot remedies on the internet. Do any of them work?

You may find websites that promise to cure your spots in as little as a week, but first you usually have to pay a small fortune and download an e-book full of spot-fixing secrets, none of which will be based on sound medical advice. Save your money.

DID YOU KNOW?

GARLIC CAN HELP TACKLE SPOTS. CUT A CLOVE OF GARLIC IN HALF AND RUB IT ON YOUR SPOTS. IT MAY STING A BIT (AND SMELL A LOT), BUT RAW GARLIC CONTAINS POWERFUL ANTI-BACTERIAL SUBSTANCES.

Spots and the pill: the science bit

Several types of contraceptive pill contain a chemical called ethynyloestroadiol (EO). This increases the levels of a substance called sex hormone-binding globulin (SHBG) in the body. This is useful because SHBG is the "binding protein" for free testosterone (the type of testosterone that provokes your oil-producing glands into overreacting), so it grabs onto the free testosterone and makes it harmless.

Dianette works particularly well because it contains not just EO but another chemical called cyproterone acetate, which prevents some of the free testosterone from acting on the sebaceous glands, so you have a double-whammy anti-free-testosterone effect.

Other contraceptive pills that are good for acne include Yasmin (which contains the ingredient drospirenone as well as EO) and Celeste and others that contain the ingredients desogestrel, drospirenone and gestodene, along with EO. But some contraceptive pills can make acne worse, including Noriday, Micronor, Norethisterone and Microgynon.

Types of spot & what you can do

Blackheads

The little back dots you get around your nose and chin. Each one is a clogged-up pore that's open at the top. The black bit isn't actually dirt, but melanin, the pigment that turns skin brown when you get a tan.

WHAT YOU CAN DO:

Steam your face to open your pores, soften the skin and loosen the plugs that keep blackheads in place.

Dry your skin and pat on a pore-cleaning strip which sticks to the blackheads more than it does to the skin. Whisk it off and it should pull the blackheads out with it.

Or, if you are careful, you can squeeze blackheads out, gently, using the pads of your fingers (don't use your fingernails; they will mark the skin and break it).

Splash your face with cold water to close up the pores, and dab on a little antiseptic.

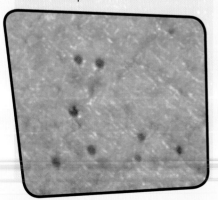

Whiteheads

If the pore is small and closed, you get a hard, lumpy little white bump – hence the name whitehead.

WHAT YOU CAN DO:

Exfoliate your skin regularly to try to unblock the pores, and avoid using any sticky or heavy creams. Don't try to extract whiteheads; they don't behave in the same way as blackheads, and if you poke at them you will push any infection around them deeper into the skin.

Papules

What a doctor would call the average red spot.

WHAT YOU CAN DO:

Keep them clean, and put on anti-spot lotion and wait for them to go away.

Acne cysts

Bigger, lumpier, more aggressive-looking spots.

WHAT YOU CAN DO:

Leave well alone and see your doctor for advice.

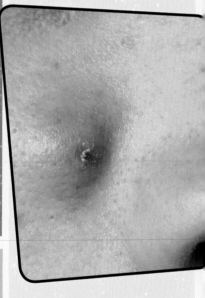

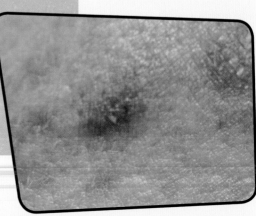

Pustules

Nasty red spots with yellow pus in them.

WHAT YOU CAN DO:

If you pick at a spot that hasn't come to a head, it will only get worse and drive the infection further into the skin, so if in doubt: LEAVE WELL ALONE.

If you absolutely have to, you can pop them, but BE CAREFUL.

Clean your face.

Warm the skin to soften it (steam your face, or have a shower).

Sterilize a needle by dipping it in boiling water.

Pierce the head of the spot.

Wrap a tissue round your fingers and GENTLY (using the pads of your fingers) squeeze the spot to push out the gunge inside.

Splash with cold water and dab with antiseptic, then leave it alone to heal.

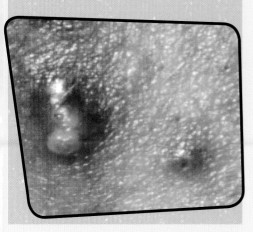

Expert tips

Dr Susan Mayou is a consultant dermatologist who has been helping people deal with problem skin for 25 years. She has three nearly grown-up children, all of whom were spotty when they were teenagers.

Why do some girls get put on the contraceptive pill to stop their acne?

After three cycles the contraceptive pill has a noticeable effect on greasy skin. But taking the pill interferes with the body's hormonal system and I don't like giving it to young girls, especially if they haven't started their periods properly.

How does it work?

Technically, what causes spots and makes skin extra greasy is a type of testosterone called "free testosterone". Some kinds of contraceptive pill, such as Dianette, counteract this "free testosterone" and therefore help clear up spots.

What is Roaccutane and is it safe? I've read that it can make people feel suicidal.

Roaccutane is the medication used for the treatment of severe acne. Don't panic if your GP or dermatologist prescribes Roaccutane – only a handful of patients find it affects their mood. For most people suffering from acne, the effects of Roaccutane can be life-changing. What it does is shrink the grease-producing glands, preventing the stickiness in the cells at the top of those glands that can lead to the glands becoming blocked. It is also anti-bacterial, so it clears up infection, and anti-inflammatory, so it calms down red, inflamed spots. My children all had courses of Roaccutane and I would never have given them anything I thought was poisonous.

Lip gloss! Eyeliner! Bring it on! I'd so love to go crazy with make-up, but my dad would go ballistic. Well, maybe I don't ALWAYS want to go crazy, but there are just so many things I'd like to try.

Make-up

Usually I want to look natural, as if I haven't really tried at all – but a bit better than normal. How do I do that? Is it possible to pull off a full-on lots-of-make-up look – with blusher and eyeshadow and proper lipstick – without looking like a clown? And how do I work out which colours suit me in the first place?

What's that on your face???

There are three reasons for wearing make-up:

✱ To feel better about yourself by looking better

✱ To cover up blemishes

✱ To make yourself look more attractive to other people

Everyone knows about the third one. The second one is pretty obvious. It's the first one that is really important – the less frivolous side of make-up, if you like. Because feeling good about yourself is a huge confidence-booster. This chapter is about how to learn the basics of make-up – what it's for, how to put it on, which colours to choose – and, above all, how to enjoy it.

There are lots of tips, too, from Louise Constad, a celebrity make-up artist who has worked on famous faces all over the world.

Q So, er, how much make-up should I wear?

That's something you will need to decide for yourself. You may have to negotiate with your mum (and dad) too. No parent is ever going to encourage you to put make-up on. And if your mum never wears the stuff, she'll be even less keen on the idea of you playing with it.

It also depends on whether you're heading for school, a party or lunch with your grandparents. And remember, there's no law that says you **have** to wear make-up at all.

What goes on first?

Smooth your complexion: cover up blotches and blemishes with concealer, tinted moisturizer or foundation

Colour your cheeks: if you're using blusher, bronzer or highlighter, this goes on next

Define your eyes: use eyeshadow, eyeliner, or just a whisk of mascara

Tint your lips: colour them, gloss them, or simply slick them with lip balm

Make-up is not an exact science. What looks great on you might not work for your friends. Here are two tips from Louise Constad which illustrate the point. They might seem to contradict each other, but they're both true:

1. Be bold: don't be afraid to try any looks that you fancy. When you're young, everything suits you, so you can get away with pretty much anything.
2. Even a little make-up can make you look totally overdone, so wear only as much as you feel comfortable with. Just because you've got eyes, doesn't mean you have to wear eyeshadow...

Foundation

None of my friends uses foundation and I look strange when I try it out. I don't want to look like a ghost.

Q What's foundation for?
It's skin-coloured make-up that you use to make your complexion look smooth and even. You probably don't need it, or at least you don't need to cover your whole face in it. Just dot it onto the areas that need it, and blend it in. Foundation comes in many different formulations, from light creamy gels to thick heavy pastes. Your best bet is a light liquid foundation that glides onto your skin and enhances it without making your face look like a mask. Tinted moisturizer does the same job with an even lighter cover. Or to hide blemishes you could just use concealer.

Q How do I pick the right colour of tinted moisturizer or concealer?
First you need to work out whether your skin tone is "warm" or "cool". This is closely, but not entirely, related to your skin colour.

Q How do I tell whether I'm warm or cool?
Try holding something gold and something silver up to your face, one after the other (it can be fabric, or jewellery). If you look closely, one will make your face look brighter and more awake; the other will make it look a bit tired and washed out. If the gold suits you better, then you have "warm" skin; if the silver is better, then you're "cool".

Q And what does the warm/cool bit mean?
✱ If you're "cool", then tinted moisturizers that are more pink than yellow will look most natural.
✱ If you're "warm", you are better off with products with a touch of yellow in them.
To test the colour, put a tiny bit on your cheek and see if it blends in.

Q Do I need powder on top?
Not unless your face is really oily and likely to go shiny in an hour or so. Face powder comes in two forms: loose in a jar, or pressed into a compact. Both give a matt finish to the skin. Wearing powder can make you look old-fashioned: most people prefer a dewy, glowing look.

How to put on powder

✱ Use a big soft brush.
✱ Dab this into the powder and tap off the excess.
✱ Dust it lightly over your cheeks, nose and forehead.

How to apply *foundation*

You can dab it on with a sponge, paint it on with a special foundation brush, or, easiest and simplest, blend it on with your fingers (their warmth helps settle it into the skin).

1 Clean your face, put on a bit of moisturizer and give that a couple of minutes to sink in before you start.

2 Dab some foundation on the centre of your face and work outwards from your nose, spreading it evenly and working it into your skin with your fingers.

Tips

Using concealer to cover up the bits that need covering looks much more natural than a full base. Dot concealer onto the areas that are bothering you (e.g. dark circles under the eyes). Then put a light moisturizer on top of the concealer – dot it on with your finger – so that it helps the concealer blend into the skin and look natural. Choose a concealer as close to your skin colour as possible (if in doubt, choose one a fraction lighter rather than a fraction darker).

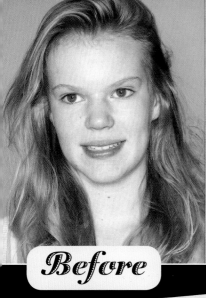

Before

After

Blusher

The trouble with blusher is that either it seems to make no difference at all, or it looks really scary. I know that it ought to give skin a nice, healthy glow, but where do you put it and how do you make it look normal? And what about finding the right colour? I don't know where to start!

Q What's it for?
What you want is a gentle flush of colour across the upper bit of your cheeks, as if you'd just done a bit of healthy exercise outdoors.

Q If I put the blusher on the apples of my cheeks, it just makes them look fatter.
Try taking the blusher away towards the edges of the face; that will stop them looking so round.

Q Can you use two colours of blusher to give yourself better cheekbones and make your nose look narrower?

How to apply blusher

It's easiest to start with a gel- or cream-based blusher.

Smile, and put a bit of blusher onto the "apples" of your cheeks (the bits that bunch up when you smile) and blend it outwards towards the edge of your face. Take a step back from the mirror and look at your whole face to see whether it's even on both sides.

How to apply powder blusher

Swirl your blusher brush around on the blusher. Tap it so that any excess powder falls off.
Smile and, starting on the smiley bits of your cheeks, sweep the colour gently over the cheeks and work out towards the hairline, blending as you go. You'll get a better result with a big, soft, round-ended blusher brush, because then you can sweep colour on, rather than scrubbing it on in patches.

You can, but it's tricky and best left to the professionals; it's too easy to end up looking strange and stripy.

Q I've read that you should put blusher on the end of your nose. Why on earth?
Actually that's a great little trick and finishes a face off nicely. Brush a bit of powder blusher or bronzer onto the tip of your nose, your chin and around your temples, where your forehead meets your hairline.

BLUSHER FACTS

WHAT KIND OF BLUSHER?

CREAM: gives a good strong colour, easy to blend

GEL: the easiest to spread and blend, usually gives a light, natural finish

LIQUID: runny lip-and-cheek tints can look very natural but are hard to control and often end up everywhere

POWDER: good controllable colour; needs a good brush for best results

WHICH COLOUR?

You need to find the one that's right for your skin tone:

YELLOW OR OLIVE SKINS do best with rosy, pinky-brown colours.

LIGHT OR MEDIUM SKIN usually suits peachy or pink colours.

DARK OR BLACK SKIN looks good with deeper, plummy or brown shades.

You'll know when you've got it right, because it just makes you look great, and a bit healthier.

Eyeshadow

I know, I know, wearing loads of eyeshadow isn't right for everyone, but I want to experiment.

Q Where does it go? I know it goes on the eyelid, but just by the eyelashes? Or all over? And how far out to the sides?

There are no rules. See what works best for you. Start by putting eyeshadow just on the actual eyelid, from the lashes up to the crease of the eyelid. See what you think. You can add a hoop of colour going up towards your eyebrows, but do it lightly or it will look garish. You could take the colour out round the outer edge of the eye and smudge a bit beneath your lower lashes. Or you could take the colour all the way up to your eyebrows.

Tip

If you're applying dark or sparkly eyeshadow, hold a tissue just below your eye. Then any stray bits of shadow will fall onto the tissue, rather than sticking on your cheek.

Q Why do some people put a dot of gold or silver eyeshadow in the inner corner of the eye?

It's a great trick. It catches the light and makes your eyes look lively and a bit further apart.

The right shadow for your eye colour

Blue eyes
Try silver (left) or bright blue (right) for very different looks. Also good: light brown (taupe), violet, bronze and gold.

Green eyes
Try a bright light green (left) or lilac and dark green (right). Also good: plums and purples, gold, browns.

Brown eyes
Try gold and purple (left) or light gold (right). Also good: almost anything, from chocolate brown to light blue.

Eyeliner

I used to worry that wearing eyeliner would make me look like a goth until I learned the trick of scribbling it into the roots of my lashes. Now I love the stuff and so do most of my friends, but we always end up doing the same thing. So we need some new ideas.

Q Which kind of eyeliner is the best?

Whichever one you find easiest to use...

Pencil eyeliner: simplest and easiest, can draw fine lines or thick lines; the best ones are soft and smudgeable

Gel eyeliner: needs to be painted on with a little brush, so a bit more fiddly, but gives a nice clean result

Liquid eyeliner: needs practice but will give a thick strong line which will stay where you've put it once it has dried

Q How do I get eyeliner to look even on both eyes?

Even make-up artists say it's hard to get it right, so take your time and practise. Or get a friend to do it for you.

Shaping eyes with *eyeliner*

✳ If your eyes are small: emphasize the outer corners of the eyes, to make them look wider. Don't ring your eyes all the way round with eyeliner as it makes them look smaller.

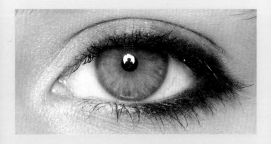

✳ If your eyes are very round the same trick works wonders to elongate the eye.

✳ Adding a touch of gold eyeliner to the inner corners of the eye adds sparkle and "wakes up" the eye.

Nine eyeliner looks to try

Natural
A thin line smudged into the upper and lower eyelashes for a bit of extra definition. Use a kohl pencil (sharpened, but not too sharp, to give a thin line).

The sixties flick
A sweeping line along the upper lid, right on the eyelashes, with an upward, outward flick at the end. Use thick, liquid eyeliner and use it boldly!

Burnt almond
Defines and exaggerates the eye. Keep the line on the inner corner of the upper lid as fine as possible and finish with a neat point at either edge of the eye.

Circus girl
Using liquid eyeliner, start by drawing a sixties flick on the upper eyelid, then repeat on the lower eyelid. Add dots and flourishes to finish off.

Hippie chick
Draw an exaggerated line out from the corner of the eye. Add flicks, dots and spots of colour wherever you like. Drawing a line of colour below the eye helps pull the colour together.

Bright and easy
As with the sixties flick, sweep a simple, clean line of bright liquid eyeliner along the upper lashes, and flick it up at the outer corner of the eye.

Ankh
A bit like an Egyptian symbol without the cross-pieces. Sketch the shape with eyeliner pencil, then finish off with liquid liner ending in a chunky, blunt-ended wing.

Colour pop
Using the brightest eyeliner pencils you can find, define the eye with a swoop of colour below the lower lashes and blended colours along the top of the lashes.

Cleopatra
Draw the lines first with thick liquid eyeliner and use a wet cotton bud to clean them up, then colour in the gap. Use a bright eye pencil, sharp enough to get a fine line.

Eyeliner tips

✱ When you're practising with eyeliner, sit down so you can rest your elbows on a table, to help keep your hands steadier.

✱ Before using a thick liquid eyeliner, sketch in the line that you want to follow with an eyeliner pencil. Once it's right, go over the line with the liquid liner.

✱ If you're blonde and/or pale-skinned, a grey, brown or green eyeliner will look less startling than black.

✱ Go easy with eyeliner inside the lower eyelid; it usually makes your eyes look smaller.

✱ When you're using liquid or gel eyeliner, let it dry before you open your eyes, otherwise you will blot your carefully-drawn line onto your upper eyelid.

✱ Give yourself enough time so that you don't have to rush. If you need to take it off, the best things for the job are a face wipe rolled into a point or a cotton bud dipped in make-up remover.

Tip

When you're putting eyeliner on with a pencil liner, pull the eyelid tight and really work the eyeliner into the base of the eyelashes. This keeps the eyeliner as close to the lashes as possible, rather than making you look as if someone has drawn rings around your eyes.

Mascara

Q How do I put mascara on without getting it everywhere?

Blot the wand on a tissue to get rid of any excess. Then, starting nearest your nose, wriggle the wand through the top lashes, stroking the mascara on from roots to tips, then do the lower lashes.

Q Do I need to use two coats of it?

Only if it's unusually thin mascara or you want a more dramatic look.

Q What if even one coat looks really startling?

You don't have to use black (which always looks a bit dramatic unless you have dark brown or black hair). There are plenty of brown or coloured mascaras around. See what looks good on you.

Tips

Before mascara dries, try holding a finger crossways near each eye and blinking both sets of lashes against it to take away any excess. You can also make your mascara look different by using coloured mascaras on the very tips of your lashes, on top of your normal mascaras.

MAKE-UP

Smoky eyes *(made simple)*

YOU WILL NEED

Eye-make-up base (not compulsory, but helps to fix the eyeshadow)

Your favourite eyeshadow

Eyeshadow brush

Old, dry, clean mascara wand

Fine eyebrow or eyeshadow brush

Eyeliner pencil

Mascara

1 Prepare the eyelids by smoothing on a dab of eye-make-up base or blotting with a damp tissue to remove oil on the skin (then eyeshadow is less likely to slide off an hour later).

2 Using the eyeshadow brush, apply your chosen colour liberally all over each eyelid, from the eyelashes to the socket line (the crease at the upper edge of the eye socket). Using a cotton bud, blend the colour upwards so that it fades towards the eyebrows, and towards the outer edge of each eye.

3 Groom the eyebrows with the old mascara wand. With the fine brush apply a little eyeshadow right below the lower lashes. Draw eyeliner along the upper eyelid for emphasis. Apply mascara. Line the inside of the lower lashes with the eyeliner. Ta-da! Smoky eyes!

Lovelier lips

I love the idea of wearing lipstick, but if I ever try it, it looks all heavy and wrong. Should I just stick to gloss?

Q Where am I going wrong with lipstick?

It's probably the colour – and the texture – that you're using. Strong red or brown, or even pink, may look too seriously grown-up, whereas purple or peach can look fresh and funky. If lipstick is heavy or waxy, it can also look too strong. Try something sheer and shiny.

Q Do I need lip-liner?

Not unless you're wearing a lipstick and want to give it a crisp edge. A hard lip line can make a face look older (not in a good way). Younger lips look better when smudged and blotted with colour.

Q Then what's lip-liner for?

To define the edges of the lips. The idea is that you draw the lip-line first, to give it a clear sharp edge, then colour in the middle with lipstick. Some people try drawing outside the natural line of their lips, to make their lips look larger. Don't. It never looks right unless it has been done by a professional make-up artist, and even then it doesn't look natural.

Q What other tricks do make-up artists use with lips?

They run a white eye pencil along the middle bit of the top lip, just outside the lip line. (If it looks odd, then smudge the edges a bit.) What this does is catch the light, and make your lips look bigger. You can also put a dab of gloss in the centre of the lower lip. This catches the light and makes the lip look fuller and fatter than it is.

Q My lips often get rough in the winter. How can I keep them smoother?

The skin on lips is very thin so they can dry out easily. Try exfoliating them very gently with an old toothbrush, then use a lip balm to help keep them moisturized.

Q Is it true that you can get addicted to lip balm?

There is a theory that if you use too much lip balm, your lips will stop being able to moisturize themselves. It's true up to a point. You don't need to smother your lips with balm the whole time. Keep it for when you need it.

Q Is it OK to use Vaseline as lip gloss? I've heard that it's really bad for you.

It's not bad for you. It's made from petroleum jelly and is very effective at protecting lips, but what it also does is form a complete

Lip tricks

Natural lips

YOU WILL NEED ✳ Lip stain or lipstick (or even blusher) ✳ A clean finger ✳ A tissue ✳ Clear gloss
Using your finger, dab the colour onto your lips. Press your lips onto the tissue to blot off any excess, so you are left with a stain of colour. Finish with gloss.

Full-on lips

YOU WILL NEED ✳ Lip-liner or lipstick and lip brush ✳ A tissue ✳ Clear gloss
Trace the outline of your lips. Use a lip pencil or lip brush for a more precise line. Fill in the colour. Blot your lips by gently pressing them onto a tissue. Add another layer of lipstick, blot again, then finish with a slick of sheer gloss.

Lipstick Queen

YOU WILL NEED ✳ Lipstick ✳ Lip brush ✳ A tissue
Using the lipstick brush to help you get a clean line around the edges of your lips, apply the lipstick. Blot, as above, by pressing your lips onto a tissue (it helps to settle the colour and the lipstick into your lips, so that it lasts longer). Paint on another layer and – voila! – vibrant lips.

barrier across them. That stops moisture escaping from the lips, but it's not so good if you want the delicate skin on your lips to be able to "breathe".

 Petroleum jelly ... er, then it's deeply un-green, isn't it?
Deeply. Petrochemicals are quite safe to use on skin but they're not remotely natural and there are plenty of alternatives out there.

Tip

When you find a look that suits you – say, strong lips, or something clever with eyeliner – try creating that look with lots of different colours to go with different outfits. It will seem as if you are doing something different each time.

Make-up for darker skin

The principles are the same, but what are the tricks and tips that make a difference?

Foundation

Find the shade that is closest to your own skin colour and use it only where you need it (under the eyes, to obscure dark circles, or to hide blemishes). What you want is for your skin to look an even tone all across your face. The darker your skin, the more foundation you can get away with and still look reasonably natural, though that's not an excuse to slap it on with a trowel. If your skin goes oily quickly, try a mattifying primer, which will help absorb oil so that make-up stays put for longer.

Blusher

Don't feel that you automatically have to reach for deep purples and plum colours, even though those may be the first choices that anyone on a make-up counter offers you. For a basic blusher, you want a colour that is two shades deeper than your own skin tone: try terracottas and browns. Red-based blushers always produce a glow, even on the darkest skin. And for a different look, try pale, baby-doll-pink blush. Your instinct will tell you it's all wrong, but it can look terrific.

Eyes

Black eyeliner suits any eyes, and any kind – from smudgy kohl to sharply defined liquid eyeliner – will look great. Using a kohl pencil on the inside of the eye will help to show off its full shape. When it comes to eyeshadow, just because bright colours show up brilliantly on your skin doesn't mean that you have to use them. Gold or dirty-bronze or gunmetal eyeshadow can look fabulous without being quite so in-your-face.

Eyebrows

If you are using an eyebrow pencil or eyeshadow to add definition to your eyebrows, don't go for black. Choose something one shade lighter than the colour of your eyebrows. It will look more natural than solid black.

Lips

You can play with darker shades of deep cherry or chocolate lip colour without looking as if your lips have shrivelled into prunes. On the other hand, be careful with bright colours; you don't want to put so much emphasis on your lips that no one notices the rest of your face. Go easy on the lip-liner, too, unless your lips are much the same colour as your skin, in which case you may want to use lip-liner just to define your mouth a bit more.

Tip

"Getting your look right, and which colours you should choose, has more to do with your personality than with the colour of your skin," says Louise. "If you're a quiet sort of person, you're never going to want to wear screamingly loud lip colours, however beautiful your face!"

Get the look

Natural

How to do a natural-but-better face

YOU WILL NEED:
Concealer or tinted moisturizer ✱ Blusher ✱ Mascara ✱ Lip gloss

1. Even out your skin tone – only if it needs it – with a thin layer of tinted moisturizer, or by covering up any spots or blotches with concealer.
2. Put a dot of blusher on the apples of your cheeks and blend it outwards and back towards the sides of your face.
3. Add a coat of mascara to your lashes.
4. Slick on some lip gloss and you're done.

How to do sparkly party make-up

YOU WILL NEED:
✱ Eye-make-up base ✱ Highlighter ✱ Sparkly or metallic eyeshadow ✱ Eyeshadow brush ✱ Coloured eyeliner ✱ Mascara ✱ Lip gloss, with just a bit of colour and a bit of sparkle in it

1. Smooth on the eye-make-up base.
2. Dab highlighter along the top of your cheekbones (smile, so that you can see the apples in your cheeks, then put the highlighter on the top bit and blend it upwards and outwards).
3. Put some highlighter just below the arch of each eyebrow, and using a finger, smooth it across that top section of the eye socket (so that your browbone catches the light).
4. Using an eyeshadow brush, apply your chosen eyeshadow to each eyelid. Put a good strong line of it close to the lashes, then use the brush to soften and blend this back towards the crease of the eyelid, and slightly out to the side of the eye. Use the brush to run a line of eyeshadow, like a thick liner, under the eye. You could even, using a finger, press little clouds of the eyeshadow around the outside edge of each eye (where the side of a pair of glasses would go).
5. Add a frame of eyeliner – but only if you think you need it. You may look striking enough already.
6. Define your lashes with mascara.
7. Gloss your lips.

Sparkly

Eyebrows

I don't want caterpillar brows, but I don't want that surprised look either.

Q **Should I pluck them? Or not?**
Only if you really need to. Don't pluck more than you have to. And read this page first.

Q **What's the best shape for eyebrows?**
A neatened-up version of your natural brow shape. Beauty magazines may go on about "creating the perfect arch", but if your brows are flat and straight, they will just look deranged if you try to force them into an arch.

Q **My eyebrows are almost invisible. What can I do?**
Colour them in! You can do this with an eyebrow pencil or, better still, with eyeshadow, applied with a small brush with a stiff rectangular end.

How to draw in stronger eyebrows

Start at the inner corner of each brow and work outwards towards the temples. Use lots of light, feathery lines, in among your existing eyebrows. This looks much more natural than drawing a solid line.

How to pluck your eyebrows

✱ Get a good pair of tweezers. Ones with slanted ends are usually easier to work with.

✱ Use a magnifying mirror if possible and a good light. Take just one hair at a time.

✱ Take hairs from alternate eyebrows (otherwise it's very hard to keep them even).

✱ Always take hairs from underneath the eyebrow, rather than above it.

✱ If in ANY doubt, take fewer rather than more. The eyebrow should start above the inner corner of the eye. If you put a pencil upright alongside your nose, between your eye and your nose, where the top of the pencil hits the eyebrow is the right place for it to start. Don't make the gap between your eyebrows wider than this; it makes your eyes look closer together.

✱ Line the pencil up from the edge of your nose, past the outside corner of your eye to where it meets the eyebrow. That's where the brow should finish. If you make brows shorter than this, it makes your eyes look smaller than they are.

✱ Don't get too hung up on making both eyebrows exactly the same. Very few people have symmetrical faces, or identical eyebrows.

Make-up housekeeping

Q **Does it really matter if I don't take my make-up off before I go to bed?**

YES! Clearly the world isn't going to end if you don't remove your mascara, but leaving your face covered with the day's dirt and bacteria plus make-up (because if you haven't bothered taking your make-up off, you won't have cleaned your face either, will you?) is not a great habit to get into. And whoever washes your pillowcase won't like it much, either.

Q **What can I do to make my make-up bag greener?**

Choose brands that are strong on more natural ingredients, and that offer recycled or recyclable containers. Reject products that

Q **How long does make-up last?**

Some of it seems to last for ever (everyone's mum has a favourite old lipstick tucked away in a drawer somewhere). But more liquid cosmetics like lip gloss and mascara make an excellent breeding-ground for bacteria (particularly the more natural brands, which contain fewer preservatives). Here's a rough guide to how long things last:

> **MASCARA:** hygiene experts say replace it every three months. It's usually fine for 6–9 months but use your common sense. If it starts to smell bad, chuck it.
> **LIQUID EYELINER:** 6–12 months
> **LIP GLOSS:** 12–18 months
> **EYESHADOW:** at least 2 years
> **LIPSTICK:** at least 2 years
> **PENCIL EYELINER:** at least 3 years

If I had my wish, I'd have an hour-glass figure and immunity to junk food... But even though I can't have everything, some things, like hair-free shins and

Bodies

softer skin, are easier to achieve. I want to know more about the serious stuff too, like animal testing, "green" cosmetics and ethical skin care. They're all better for the world, but which are better for my body?

Moisturize

Unless you are really lucky, your skin will need a bit of help to keep it soft and smooth.

Q My skin is always dry. How can I keep it softer?

You need to trap moisture in the skin to keep it soft and smooth, so after you have a bath or shower, put on plenty of moisturizer, body butter or body oil once you are roughly dry, BEFORE your skin has dried out completely. That will help to seal in a bit of the water that has been on your skin. Also, eat plenty of foods containing omega-3 essential fatty acids, such as seeds and oily fish. They help prevent water loss from the skin by keeping the membrane of the skin cells intact.

Q Soap or shower gel which is best?

Whichever you like. Both will get you clean – but both will interfere with the skin's protective barrier and leave your skin feeling a bit dry. But you don't have to use either. You could just wash with water, or rub yourself down with oil before you get into the bath or shower, then rinse it off (watch out, it may get slippery). If you're covered in mud or feel really smelly, then of course you'll need something like shower gel to help get yourself clean.

Q How do I get my back clean? I don't want it to get spotty but it's hard to reach.

Try a long-handled, soft back-brush, or use something like a Japanese wash cloth, a long thin scarf of loosely-woven nylon. You can flip it behind your back, hold both ends and then pull it back and forth.

Q Are some shower gels better than others? I was given one as a present and it gave me a rash...

I bet it was a cheap and highly fragranced one. Fragrance (often just called "parfum" on the label) is the first thing that's likely to cause a reaction. The second is sodium lauryl sulphate (SLS) or, to a slightly lesser extent, its close cousin sodium laureth sulphate (SLES). These ingredients are detergents,

Tip

In order to use less shower gel and to make it last longer, get a body-puff made from lots of scrunched-up bits of net. Wet it, then put a tiny bit of shower gel on it and rub it about. The gel will froth up into heaps and heaps of foam.

which means they cut through grease, and they are what make shampoo, toothpaste and shower gel foam up when you use them. SLS is also well known to irritate the skin. So if it makes your skin react, try to avoid it.

Q Why do they put it in stuff if it's an irritant?

It's cheap and effective and most people can tolerate it, as it is washed off straight away. It can be more irritating in bubble bath if you soak in it for hours.

Q How can I stop my elbows and knees from getting dry and scaly? And what about those tiny bumps down my arms?

Exfoliate them gently when you are in the bath or shower, and moisturize them lots and lots. It's really hard to keep these areas soft, particularly as they don't have many oil glands, so they need all the help you can give them.

Exfoliate

Scuffing off dead skin feels good and helps your skin to glow.

Q **What is exfoliating?**
Exfoliating is polishing off the outermost skin cells which are actually already dead but still sticking on to the skin. Do it when your skin is damp, using a body scrub (make your own – the recipes here are great) or lather up a pair of stretchy, slightly scratchy exfoliating gloves with shower gel. Or try body-brushing. Once the dead cells are removed, your skin will feel smoother and any oils or moisturizers you use afterwards will sink into your skin more evenly.

Q **So what's body-brushing? It sounds like something you'd do with horses.**
Well, it's not that different. A body-brush is made with stiff natural bristles and often has a long handle to make it easier to reach up and down your legs and arms. Body-brushing is a really good beauty habit to get into because it boosts the immune system, too, by helping the body's lymphatic drainage system to do its job and clear out bacteria and viruses from your bloodstream.

How to body-brush

This is something you need to do when your skin is properly dry, so do it before a bath or shower, rather than afterwards.

1 Start at your feet and work upwards, towards your heart.

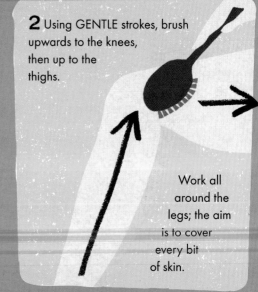

2 Using GENTLE strokes, brush upwards to the knees, then up to the thighs.

Work all around the legs; the aim is to cover every bit of skin.

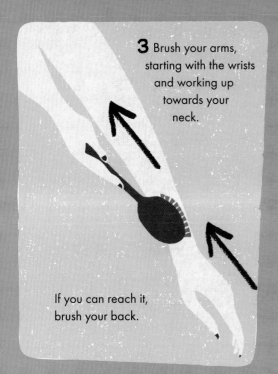

3 Brush your arms, starting with the wrists and working up towards your neck.

If you can reach it, brush your back.

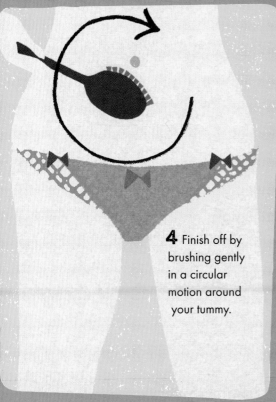

4 Finish off by brushing gently in a circular motion around your tummy.

Make your own body scrubs

Sugar scrub

Sugar and salt are both great natural exfoliants, but larger bits of rock salt can be scratchy, so start with sugar.

YOU WILL NEED
2 handfuls granulated or caster sugar
Olive oil to mix
A couple of drops of your favourite
    aromatherapy oil or perfume

1 Stir the ingredients together in a bowl to form a sludgy mixture.
2 When your skin is damp, use the scrub to rub off all those dead skin cells.

Oatmeal scrub

Oatmeal is very soothing for sensitive or easily irritated skin and helps to keep skin moist by leaving a thin film of oat proteins on the surface.

YOU WILL NEED
2 handfuls oats
Water or olive oil to mix

1 Blitz the oats in a blender until very fine.
2 Mix in a bowl with water or oil until they form a sloppy paste.
3 Rub the paste gently over damp skin, concentrating on rough areas like elbows and knees. Rinse well.
WARNING: This mixture may turn into sticky lumps of porridge when washed down the plug hole. Be careful not to block up the plumbing system!

Hair removal

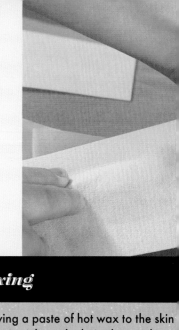

If your body hair doesn't bother you, that's great, and you can skip all this. But for the rest of us, well. Where do I start? When I first wanted my legs to look smooth I tried hair-removal cream: disgusting/messy, but it worked. Then I tried waxing – not too painful – but the simplest for me is shaving.

	Shaving	**Hair-removal cream**	**Waxing**
WHAT IS IT?	Removing the hair with a razor.	Cream that dissolves the hair at its roots. Smear it over the hair you want to be rid of, wait a few minutes, then wipe off.	Applying a paste of hot wax to the skin so that it sticks to the hair, then sticking a strip of cloth onto the wax and ripping it, the wax and the hairs, all off.
PRO	Quick, easy, can be done in the shower.	Cheap, quite quick, not difficult.	Great, clean result. Removes hair at the roots so it lasts for up to six weeks.
CON	Also easy to nick your skin. Doesn't last long. Hair grows back stubbly.	The cream always smells and it's messy. Often gets really itchy while it's working.	Can hurt really quite a lot, depending on how well it's done. You can't wax again until the hair is long enough to remove (about four to six weeks).
NEED TO KNOW	Change your razor regularly. Use shave gel, shaving oil, shower gel or even conditioner so that the blade moves smoothly over your skin.	Do the patch test first, as it suggests on the packet. You just might be allergic to one of the ingredients, and it's better to have a tiny red patch than two red legs. Don't leave it on too long; the chemicals that get rid of the hair can cause serious skin irritation. Don't get it on your mum's best towels, as it may leave marks.	If you're worried about how much it is going to hurt, take a painkiller like paracetamol a couple of hours beforehand. And don't book a wax just before your period; you will be feeling a bit more sensitive and it will hurt much more than usual.

Epilator	Threading	Laser hair removal	Electrolysis
A hand-held gadget like an electric razor, with rotating blades that grab hairs and tweak them out.	Pulling out individual hairs using a cat's cradle of cotton threads.	Zapping hairs with laser light or intense pulsed light (IPL) to destroy the hair right down to the root in its follicle.	Applying a needle with an electric current running through it to each hair, to destroy the hair at its root.
Easy to use, removes hair from roots so results last well.	Really quick; great for shaping eyebrows and removing upper-lip hairs.	Can lead to a permanent reduction in the amount of hair you have.	Will deal with hair more or less permanently; can be used on the face.
Not exactly pain-free, not good for underarms.	Less practical for larger expanses of hair.	Very expensive (seriously, we're talking in £100s per session) and you need lots of sessions for best results.	Very slow (to clear one forearm might take a year of weekly visits) and very expensive (more £100s).
Some models are much less painful than others. Really hurts on more sensitive areas (e.g. bikini line and armpits).	You need to find a skilled practitioner. It's not something you can try at home and bear in mind that your eyebrows may look red and sore afterwards.	The darker your hair and the fairer your skin, the better the result. Won't work on blonde hair, or if your skin is dark.	Not as quick or effective as laser or IPL hair removal; needs more than one session. Less popular now that laser and IPL treatments are on offer; more often used for removing hairs on the face.

Q The skin on my legs always gets really dry after I've shaved them. What can I do about it?

Your skin, particularly on your shins, can often feel drier after shaving. Moisturize regularly to soften it up.

Q Why does hair grow back stubbly after you've shaved?

Because the razor cuts cleanly across the hair (imagine slicing a knife across a carrot, slightly on the diagonal). When that sharply sliced end of the hair grows away from the skin, it will feel rough. Whatever people tell you, shaving doesn't make hair grow back stronger, darker or faster.

Q How do you avoid getting ingrown hairs after shaving?

Exfoliate regularly. Removing dead skin cells that are sticking onto the top of the skin can help ingrown hairs bust their way back out. Keeping skin soft and moisturized helps, too.

Q Does waxing really weaken hair and make it grow back more slowly?

When you've waxed, the hairs have been ripped out by the roots, so they've got to start all over again. The first bits that emerge

Tip

Don't shave dry skin, you'll get a "razor burn" rash.

through your skin will be little soft new ends which will seem finer and softer, but then they will carry on growing just like before.

Q After things like waxing and laser hair removal, what can you put on the skin to calm it down?

Aloe vera gel, the purer the better, is great and very soothing, or a body lotion with antiseptic tea-tree oil in it. If you've had laser treatments, the clinic should give you a special skin-calming gel to help reduce redness and irritation.

Q What about the red bumps you get after waxing?

If bumps appear immediately after waxing, they should calm down by the end of the day. But if they are big and red and angry-looking, then it might be folliculitis, which is an infection of the hair follicles, and you should see your doctor for medication to help clear it up.

Q Are there any permanent ways of removing hair?

Not that are guaranteed. Laser or intense pulsed light systems usually promise only to bring about a "permanent reduction" in the amount of hair, rather than to get rid of it for good.

Sweat & smells

OK, none of us wants body odour. Here's how to stay smelling sweet.

Q **Why do armpits smell?**
Well, you have a whole bunch of sweat glands in your armpits, and because your arms spend most of their time hanging down at your side, when you sweat the entire area gets damp. Your sweat doesn't smell, but once it is trapped in your armpit, it starts to fester a bit and then is eaten by the bacteria that live on your skin (yes, sorry, it's all a bit "eeuww"!), and that's what produces the smell.

Q **Why does armpit sweat smell worse than sweat on your back?**
You have two types of sweat glands. The eccrine glands produce watery sweat all over your body to cool you down. The others, the apocrine glands in the armpits, produce much less sweat, but this is the stuff that smells.

Q **Phew! So why do some people's armpits smell worse than others?**
A. It depends on how often you wash.
B. It depends on whether or not you use deodorant or antiperspirant.
C. Because that's life. Some people hardly smell at all, whereas others...

Q **Why do some people seem to have no idea that they smell really awful?**
Probably because none of us really notices smells that are always there. Most of us can't tell whether or not we smell without actually sticking our noses into our armpits.

Q **Do hairy armpits smell more than shaved ones?**
They do, just because the more hair there is, the faster the sweat becomes smelly.

Tip
Wash your armpits with shower gel or shampoo. It works better than soap, because armpit sweat has oils in it, and shower gel and shampoo dissolve oil better than soap does.

Q **OK, what's the best way NOT to have smelly armpits?**
Wash regularly. This gets rid of old smells and also keeps down the levels of bacteria. Use a

deodorant to counteract any
new smells that might develop.

Q **What's the difference between a deodorant and an antiperspirant?**
One stops you smelling and
the other stops you sweating.
Most underarm products are
designed to do both.

Q **Isn't it a bad idea to prevent your body from sweating?**
It's not natural to stop your
body from sweating. But it's not
harmful to the body.

Q **Are there any nice safe natural things I can try instead?**
Deodorant crystals. These are
lumps of crystal salts which
you dampen, then wipe across
your armpits. They work like
an antiperspirant, by leaving
a film of mineral salts across
your armpit which cut down the
amount you sweat and tackle
the smell, too, though not as
effectively as a chemical-based
product would.

Deodorant

Is it good? Is it bad? Here's the essential info.

Q What's the fuss over antiperspirants and deodorants?

There are two kinds of ingredients used in deodorants and antiperspirants that have been a cause for concern:

✱ **Aluminium salts** (e.g. aluminium chlorohydrate and aluminium zirconium tetrachlorohydrex GLY), which are used in antiperspirants to reduce sweating.

✱ **Parabens** (e.g. methylparaben and butylparaben), which are used as preservatives in the vast majority of cosmetics.

The concerns over aluminium salts are:

✱ that they block the body's sweat glands and so stop your body from being able to sweat out toxins.

✱ that they are absorbed into the body and may accumulate and damage the DNA of the body's cells, and cause cancer. One study, which looked at cancerous breast tissue, found it had high levels of aluminium in it. Did this come from antiperspirants? It hasn't been scientifically proved, and leading authorities such as Cancer Research UK say that there is no link between antiperspirants and cancer, but it has raised a lot of questions.

The worry with parabens is:

✱ that they might imitate the things that the hormone oestrogen does in the body. So far, studies have been inconclusive.

✱ that they might be linked to breast cancer. A research study in 2004 found parabens in samples of breast tissue taken from women with breast cancer. Did they come from deodorants? This idea – that the body absorbed parabens through the skin of the armpit and settled in the breast, disturbing the DNA of the cells and causing cancer – grabbed all the headlines. What didn't get so much attention were the serious questions raised afterwards about the way this study was done. Scientists have now dismissed the study's alarming suggestions.

Our bodies absorb far more parabens from the food we eat than we ever could pick up from preservatives in body products. Scientists also point out that it's hard to imagine how a substance would get from the armpit into the breast, given that the blood flow in the body works the other way round.

Tip

Wearing cotton clothes keeps armpits fresher than wearing man-made fibres because natural fibres allow more air circulation.

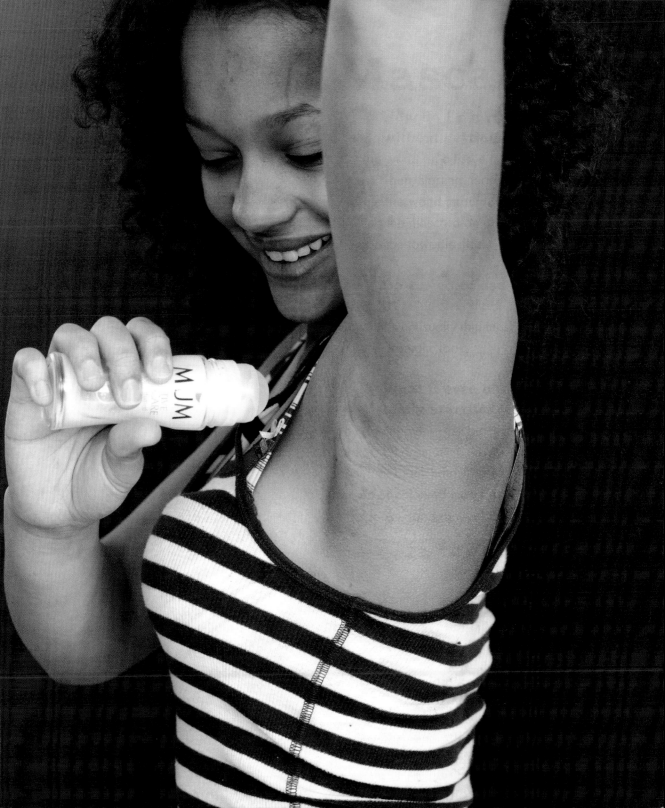

What's green?

So what makes a product green? And does it mean it's better for us?

Q Is it true that skin absorbs 60 per cent of what's put on it, so lots of ingredients in body products end up in your bloodstream and can make you toxic?

For starters, a thick oil or balm won't stand a chance of being absorbed (your skin will stay all greasy). Even though a lighter body lotion will be absorbed right into the skin's many layers, its ingredients are unlikely to pass right through the skin. The skin's main function is as a barrier between your body and the outside world (we don't swell up as a result of absorbing lots of water when we get into a bath, though it does soften up the top layers of the skin). So it's unlikely although not impossible that some ingredients will go a bit further.

Q But some medicines go into the body through patches, so why don't cosmetics?

Scientists say that it's quite tricky to get the body to absorb drugs through the skin and that if it was a really good way of getting substances into the body there would be many more medicines available as patches rather than pills.

Q But can these things stack up in your body in some sort of toxic cocktail and make you ill?

The answer depends on who you talk to. People in the natural camp will tell you that the toxic-cocktail effect is very real; that our bodies absorb a great deal of the products that we slather over them and that it can all

be bad for our general health. Scientists and toxicologists, on the other hand, say that the toxic-cocktail effect is one of the bigger modern beauty myths. They will point out that very little of what we ladle onto our skin is absorbed any further than into the outer layers of the skin; that our bodies are generally very good at dealing with, and getting rid of, any substances that shouldn't be in them; and that many of the alarming-sounding toxic substances that are found in the human body have got there as a result of environmental pollution, or through the food that we eat, rather than from our shampoo or body lotion. Which view should you believe? It's one of the tricky modern issues on which you'll have to make up your own mind.

Q I'm still worried...

Then choose body products that have a high proportion of natural or organic ingredients.

Q Are products that say they are "natural" better for my skin than ones that are full of chemicals?

Not necessarily, though they are likely to be better from an environmental point of view and possibly more ethically produced and sourced.

Q What about organic skin-care products? They're often more expensive...

You need to read the labels carefully. Most serious organic skin-care products will have a stamp of approval from the Soil Association or Ecocert, which shows that the product comprises either 70 per cent, or 95 per cent organic ingredients.

Q How do I know if a "natural" skin-care product is really that natural?

The serious natural-skin-care companies all aim to avoid using certain ingredients in their products. Take a look at the ingredients list. Things that natural-skin-care products should be free from include:
Parabens
Petrochemicals
Artificial colours
Synthetic fragrance
Sodium lauryl/laureth sulphate

Q What's so bad about these?

Parabens are preservative ingredients which have been labelled as carcinogens – substances that can lead to cancer.
Petrochemicals form a protective layer of oil over the skin, which covers the pores and makes it hard for the skin to breathe.
Artificial colours can irritate the skin.
Synthetic fragrance can also irritate the skin.
Sodium lauryl/laureth sulphate are ingredients that help shampoo, bubble bath and toothpaste to foam up when you use them. They can irritate the skin.

Get ethical

Eco-friendly products that aren't tested on animals are the way forward.

Q What is ethical skin care?

Making beauty products more ethical is a huge issue in the beauty industry. "Ethical" covers a wide variety of concerns: it means choosing basic ingredients that have been grown in a sustainable way, paying a fair price for them, making products in a way that doesn't harm the environment, cutting down the amount of packaging used, making that packaging recyclable and, crucially, refusing to test products or ingredients on animals.

This hasn't been a priority for beauty companies in the past, but finally that is changing, which is good news. Awareness of ethical issues has grown fast, particularly in the UK. Consumers – that's all of us who buy these things – are demanding products that are eco-friendly and don't harm animals or other people's lives, and the companies that make them are responding. In 2007, the UK and France produced 75 per cent of the 2,260 ethical cosmetics that were launched in Europe.

How can you help this along? Choose products from companies that have good ethical credentials. Vote with your purse by avoiding companies that don't measure up to good ethical standards.

Q How do I know if products have been tested on animals?

It is against European Union law to test any cosmetic products on animals – which sounds good, but there are various loopholes. Some companies avoid animal testing but still use ingredients that are tested on animals elsewhere in the world where it is not illegal. And there are other exemptions that animal-rights groups are unhappy about – like the fact that if ingredients need to be checked for toxicity, or for whether they might affect a person's fertility, they can legally be tested on animals until 2013 (and possibly after that, if scientists don't find an alternative). If you want to know what a company's policy is on this, the best way to find out is to get in touch. Call or email their customer services and demand an answer.

Expert tips for green teen beauty queens

-- -- -- -- -- -- -- -- -- -- -- -- -- -- -- -- -- --

From Charlotte Vøhtz, founder of the Green People Company Ltd

❊ Choose organic mineral make-up where possible; a good tip is to choose a high-organic-content moisturizer and mix this with a mineral powder to create your own kinder foundation, also meaning you can match the perfect colour for your skin tone!

❊ Make organic choices where it matters more. Experiment with the products that promise longer lashes and fuller lips, but stock up on organic staples such as a quality moisturizer and cleanser.

❊ Replace your chemical-laden body lotion and shower gel for organic alternatives.

From Sarah Stacey and Josephine Fairley, authors of The Green Beauty Bible

❊ Start thinking in terms of "beauty miles"; how far has a product had to travel to reach you? Choose things that are made closer to home.

❊ Consider making your own beauty products.

❊ Avoid extra packaging, particularly if it's made of plastic, wherever possible.

❊ Use filtered tap water (because there are so many chemicals in normal tap water) both for drinking and for cooking – then you needn't buy plastic bottles of water. These are often imported, and toxic chemicals have been shown to leach out of the plastic, especially when it's warm.

❊ Avoid petrochemicals – you'll find them listed as ingredients such as "petrolatum" or "mineral oil". They're derived from minerals, which are fossil fuels, and the world is running out of them. There are loads of great natural alternatives.

❊ Keep your beauty regime as simple and natural as you can: you don't want skin care products with too many synthetic ingredients in them. One way is to choose products with as few ingredients as possible.

❊ Try to think in terms of swapping rather than buying. If you have colours of eyeshadow or nail varnish that aren't great on you, see if your friends would like them. (But don't swap anything liquid that you have used, like mascara or lip gloss, as you'll just be passing on the old bacteria which are brewing up in there...)

❊ Follow the three Rs: Reduce, Re-use and Recycle. Reduce the number of products that you buy. Re-use the pots and bottles that cosmetics come in. Recycle the packaging.

❊ Ask cosmetics companies what they are doing to make their products greener and more eco-friendly. Send them an email and ask what their policies are on green issues or the environment.

Skin & sun

I love getting outside in the sunshine. It feels so good and I long to get a tan. But if there's one thing Mum goes on about more than brushing teeth, it's wearing sunscreen. Not just on holiday, but **EVERY** day, even when it's not sunny. When I groan, Mum says that if I'd spent as much time talking to dermatologists as she has, I wouldn't even ask. But I still love getting outside in the sunshine, so how can I enjoy the sun without doing my skin harm?

Sun, sun, sun

It feels good to be out in the sunshine, but you need to treat those rays with respect.

Q What's so wrong with getting a tan?

Getting a tan really isn't good for the skin.

Q How come?

A tan is the skin's way of protecting itself when it's been exposed to the sun's ultraviolet rays. So a tan is a sign of damage that has already been done to the skin.

Q A tan doesn't last very long. Can't the skin repair itself?

It can, but deep down it remembers what's happened and the effects of all those ultraviolet rays add up over a lifetime.

Q But lots of older people have been tanning all their lives and they seem fine...

Yes, but 25 years ago we didn't know better. Now

scientists have proved beyond any doubt that the main cause of ageing in the skin is exposure to ultraviolet light.

Q So, you get wrinkles. Everyone gets wrinkles!

The other problem is skin cancer, which is a direct result of too much ultraviolet light. The number of people who get skin cancer in the UK each year has doubled over the past 20 years (it's now close to 70,000), and British children and teenagers have the highest rates of skin cancer of any European country.

Q Why do people wear sunscreen when it's not sunny?

Because UVA rays, which age the skin, are around whenever it's daylight. Scientists reckon that we get 70 per cent of our lifetime sun exposure before the age of 17. This means that whatever damage is being done to your skin happens early on in your life. You might think you're not outside that much, but if you think about all the time you've ever spent playing in the garden, on holiday at the beach, in sports lessons, etc., you can see it all adds up. The easiest way to protect your skin is to wear a moisturizer with sunscreen in it every day and then forget about it.

DID YOU KNOW?

UVA RAYS TRAVEL THROUGH GLASS. SO IF YOU'RE SITTING IN THE CAR ON A SUNNY DAY, OR IF YOU HAVE A DESK BY THE WINDOW, THEY CAN STILL REACH YOU.

UV rays

The sun gives us light and warmth; but the lighter your skin, the more damage the sun's invisible ultraviolet rays can do. There are two types of ultraviolet rays that affect the skin:

UVA – the ageing ones

These are around whenever it is daylight. They don't cause any immediate damage, but they slowly destroy the collagen – the stuff that forms the structure of skin cells – beneath the skin's surface. So everything looks fine until your late twenties, but then the damage starts to show up in the form of rapidly increasing lines, wrinkles and, eventually, brown spots of pigmentation.

UVB – the burning ones

These are the ones that cause redness, burning and, yes, tanning. They're strongest when the sun is highest in the sky (between 11 a.m. and 3 p.m.), and they're stronger in the summer, the nearer you go to the Equator, and the higher you go up a mountain. They're more powerful on clear, sunny days, but they reach through cloud, too.

How strong is the UV light today?

Check the UV index on the weather forecast.

Sunscreen

It's very simple: you have to wear it. Then you can get on with the rest of your life.

Q What's the best way to avoid sunburn?

The best advice is to follow the SMART code. It's all about having a healthy respect for the sun and what it can do.

Q What do the ratings on sunscreen bottles mean?

SPF refers to how much protection the product gives against UVB rays. If your skin usually starts to burn after you've been in the sun for five minutes, then using SPF 15 means you should be able to be in the sun for 15 times as long (15 x 5 mins) before you start to burn.

The number of stars shows how good a product is at protecting from UVA rays. Three stars is reasonable, four stars is good, five is the best.

Q Do I really need to wear factor 15?

Yes, you do! But you don't need anything higher than that, unless you are hanging about on a beach, or doing watersports on a

The SunSmart Code

S pend time in the shade between 11 a.m. and 3 p.m.

M ake sure that you never burn.

A im to cover up with a T-shirt, hat and sunglasses.

R emember that children should take extra care in the sun.

T hen use sunscreen with SPF 15 or higher.

sunny holiday abroad. SPF 15 blocks up to 94 per cent of UVB rays. That's most of them. SPF 30 blocks up to 96 per cent and SPF 50, 98 per cent – not a huge increase.

Also, higher-factor creams tend to be more expensive, and because you feel more "protected" with a higher-factor cream you'll be tempted to stay out in the sun for longer or leave it longer before you apply more.

Q Why do I need to keep reapplying sunscreen?

Because as you move around, swim, rub yourself down with towels and put on or take off clothing, it will slightly rub off. Also, in most sunscreens, the ingredients that provide the protection start to break down once they are exposed to the sunlight.

Mineral or chemical sunscreen?

	Mineral	Chemical
Made from	Ground-up minerals such as titanium dioxide and zinc oxide.	High-tech chemical sunscreen ingredients such as Mexoryl and oxybenzone.
How they work	The minerals act as a barrier to reflect the sun's rays away from the skin.	The active ingredients absorb the UV rays and stop them damaging the skin.
Benefits	If you're allergic to other sunscreens, these may be better, but they may look white and chalky on the skin.	There's a huge range to choose from, so you're bound to find one with a smell and texture that you like in your price range.

How much sunscreen do you need to use?

Follow the two-finger rule. Squeeze out sunscreen along the length of your first two fingers. Use this much sunscreen on each of these parts of your body:

EACH UPPER LEG (BACK AND FRONT)

CHEST

upper back

lower back

EACH ARM

Face, neck and ears

EACH LOWER LEG (BACK AND FRONT)

STOMACH

If you use less, you won't be getting the amount of protection indicated on the bottle.

Sunburn & skin cancer

These are the things you don't want to think about, but which you need to know.

Q What if I do get sunburned?
Your skin will be red and sore, so you need to try to cool it down. A cold shower will help temporarily, then pat on a soothing, cooling after-sun lotion, or even natural yogurt. (If you're abroad, you may be able to find a sunburn spray that contains local anaesthetic.) If your skin is badly burned or blistered, ask a pharmacist or your doctor for advice. Take paracetamol to help with the pain.

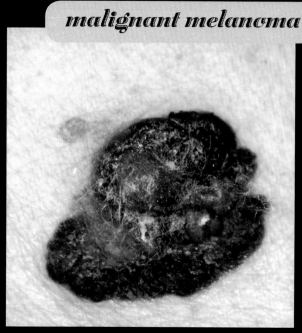
malignant melanoma

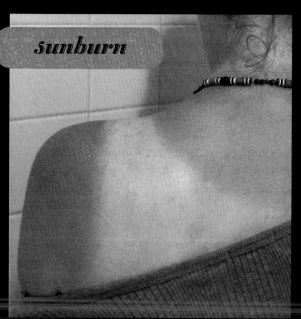
sunburn

Q How deadly is skin cancer?
It depends on what kind it is. There are two main types of skin cancer:
✱ Non-melanoma cancers such as "basal cell carcinoma" and the "squamous cell carcinoma" are rarely fatal, but they still require surgery to remove the tumours from the skin.
✱ Malignant melanomas are much more dangerous unless they are diagnosed early and treated quickly. They kill around 1,500 people in the UK each year.

Q I've got loads of moles! Eek! How do I know whether they're normal or if it's skin cancer?

Use the five-point ABCDE check below, as recommended by the British Association of Dermatologists. If you're in any doubt, see your GP and ask to get referred to a consultant dermatologist.

Asymmetry – the two halves of the area may differ in shape (moles are usually symmetrical).

Border – the edges of the area may be irregular or blurred, and sometimes show notches (moles usually have smooth edges).

Colour – anything that has different shades of black, brown and pink in the same area could be a problem (most moles are just one colour).

Five-point mole check

Diameter – most melanomas (cancerous moles) are at least 6mm in diameter. Anything that is increasing in size or shape should be shown to your doctor (normal moles tend to stay as they are, and don't suddenly expand).

Expert – if in doubt, check it out! If your GP is concerned about your skin, make sure you see a consultant dermatologist, an expert who can diagnose skin cancer. Your GP can refer you via the NHS.

How to make fake tan look like the real thing

1 Exfoliate gently all over whichever part of you you're planning to fake-tan, and shower.

2 Moisturize the drier bits of your skin that otherwise will absorb too much of the fake tan and go too dark. That means elbows, wrists, knees, ankles and toes.

3 Put on the fake-tan lotion. To make sure you don't miss any patches, start with one leg, say, and work all the way up to the top, then do the other leg, then your arms one at a time. It's much easier to see where the fake tan's going if you use one that has a "guide colour" because it will show up brown on the skin. This means you'll notice any patches you've forgotten.

4 Scrub your hands thoroughly afterwards with a nail-brush and liquid soap, or wash your hands with exfoliator, to avoid yellow-stained hands. If you think you're going to end up doing this a lot, it's worth investing in a box of latex gloves (about £10 for 100 pairs). They're thin and stretchy so you can feel what you're doing, even if using them does feel rather strange.

5 Ideally, put fake tan on in the evening and let yourself dry off properly before you get into bed. If it's daytime, don't wear anything light or tight for the first few hours (the colour will rub off on your clothes, and leave you with funny-patterned marks).

For quick, instant colour, try a bronzing gel that you can wash off at the end of the day. Wipe on, let it dry, and off you go. They're great for doing legs quickly and if it looks awful, you can wash it straight off.

If you're trying out an airbrush tan-in-a-can, stand on a dark towel before you start spraying.

Tip

Unless you want to turn really tanned overnight, you might do best with one of the many gradual-tan moisturizers which give you just a bit of colour so you can slap them on without worrying too much about whether you missed a patch.

Sunbeds – why they are a really bad idea

✱ Like the sun, tanning beds and booths provide a direct dose of ultraviolet rays which can damage the DNA in skin cells; this can in time make the skin look wrinkly and older than it really is and can even lead to skin cancer.

✱ These damaging rays have even more of an effect on young skin than on older skin.

✱ In Scotland, it is against the law for anyone under 18 to use sunbeds. With any luck, that law will soon be extended to the rest of the UK.

If there's one bit of pampering that I love, it's a manicure. I know that having my nails painted won't improve my school grades or help bring about world peace, but it's a great way to cheer myself up. Looking after your hands and feet doesn't

Hands & feet

have to take much time. I mean, how long does it take to cut your toenails? I never even think about my feet unless they look really gross – at least, not until it's summer.

Look after your hands and feet

A little TLC goes a long way towards keeping your hands and feet in good shape.

Q What's the best shape for nails?

Toenails should be cut straight across; fingernails can be whatever shape you prefer – rounded, square or oval.

Q I'm right-handed, so how do I cut the nails on my right hand?

Just keep practising. But until you can do it, try using a small pair of nail-clippers. These cut in a straight line, so you will have to work around the nail, chipping bits off. Then file the nails to get rid of any rough edges.

Q Can't I just file my nails instead?

Yes, if you have the patience. File them from the sides towards the middle rather than just scrubbing the file back and forth (that may be quicker but it weakens the nail and leaves it looking rough and frayed).

Q What's a nail-buffer?

A buffer is for polishing the nail to make it shine. With your nails clean and dry, you need to rub the buffer quickly back and forth across the surface of the nail. Don't press too hard, just get the buffer moving quite fast and your nails should soon start to gleam.

Q How does it do that?

It's basically sanding down the surface of the nail to get it smooth and shiny – so you don't want to do it too much, especially if your nails are on the weak side, because it may make them thinner and weaker.

How to have beautiful soft feet (and hands)

1 File away any hard bits of dead skin with a foot file.
2 Have a bath, relax and soak your feet.
3 Apply a thick layer of your gungiest body cream or foot cream.
4 Pull on a pair of socks (thin cotton socks if you have them, so your feet won't get too hot).
5 Go to sleep.
In the morning, your feet will be gorgeously soft.

This trick works with hands, too. Obviously you don't need to tackle your hands with a file or soak them; just put on a thick layer of cream, then pull on a thin pair of cotton gloves. Not many people have these around the house unless they've been given a hand-pampering kit as a present; you can use a pair of socks instead (yes, it feels a bit odd, but the extra warmth helps the cream to work its way right into the skin).

Nail problems

They split, they peel, they break... When nails need extra help, here's what you need to know.

Q **How do I stop biting my nails?**
First, you've got to really, really want to stop biting them. Nail-biting is a bad habit, and habits take a while to break or change. You need to try to work out why you're snacking on your nails in the first place. Is it because you are bored? Or is it something you do when you are stressed or anxious? If you can work out when and why you're doing it, it makes it that much easier to catch yourself doing it and then to stop.

Things to try

* Painting nails with disgusting-tasting anti-biting potions
* Chewing gum, to keep your mouth busy
* Treats/bribery. Persuade your mum that you deserve a reward if you can manage to stop for a day/week/month
* Hypnosis – seriously. If nothing else works, try a self-help tape, or seek professional advice

Nail gallery

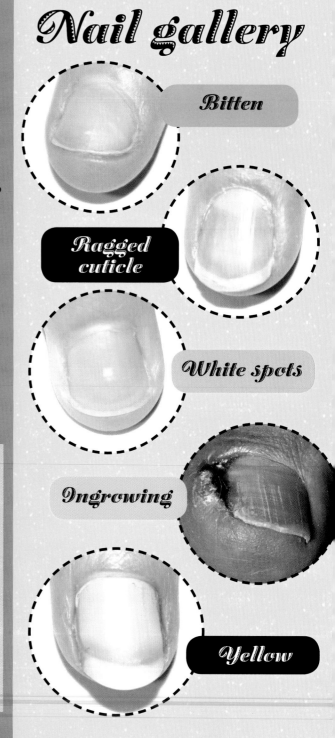

Bitten

Ragged cuticle

White spots

Ingrowing

Yellow

Q How can I make my nails stronger? If they ever grow, they're all weak and then they split.
It might be that your diet is short on minerals, trace elements and other micronutrients such as copper, manganese, chromium, zinc and iodine. You need only eat tiny amounts of these to make a big difference to the condition of nails (and your hair, too). Make sure that you are eating well (that means lots of fresh fruit and vegetables, and enough protein such as meat, fish, cheese and eggs). You could try taking one of the special skin, hair and nails vitamin supplements, and try some of the nail-hardening formulas that you can paint onto your nails like a polish. It's not a great idea to keep your nails covered in chemicals the whole time, but these can help make the nail stronger on the outside while they're getting healthier from the inside out.

Q Why do I get white spots in my nails? Someone told me I needed more calcium, but I eat plenty of yogurt and that's got calcium in it.
It's a lack of zinc, rather than calcium, that leads to white flecks in your nails. You get zinc from foods like meat and fish; if you don't eat so much of these (or if you are vegetarian), it makes sense to take a vitamin supplement that has 15 micrograms of zinc in it, at least until the problem clears up.

Q How can I stop my cuticles getting all ragged?
Cuticles need all the help you can give them. So, whenever you get a chance, rub some hand cream or nail oil into them and push them gently back off the nails. This is easier when they're damp and soft, after a bath or shower. If they are hanging in strips, you can cut these off with a cuticle-nipper – but do it carefully; the blades of these nippers tend to be really sharp.

Q Why do nails go yellow?
It's usually because they've been stained by having strong-coloured nail varnish on them for too long. That's why you're supposed to wear a base coat – it's not just because they're trying to sell you another product.

Q What causes ingrown toenails?
Wearing too-tight shoes or cutting toenails down at the edges (rather than straight across). Ingrown nails are painful and need to be fixed by a qualified chiropodist or podiatrist.

How to paint your nails

Paint your nails perfectly every time!

1 Rest the hand that you're painting firmly on a surface (desk, table, kitchen worktop) and steady the hand that is holding the brush by resting that elbow on the surface, too.

2 Dip the brush in the pot, and then wipe off any excess; you don't want it dripping. Put one stroke of varnish down one side of the nail, one down the other, then a final one straight down the middle of the nail, to join them up. For a professional finish, take the varnish over the ends of the nail tips and put a smidgen on the undersides of the nails, to "seal" the nail tip.

3 Let each layer of varnish dry before you do the next one. If possible, leave 10 minutes between each coat of polish. That way, the varnish dries as you go along. Multiple layers take much longer to dry out.

4 Add a layer of top coat (clear nail varnish). It may seem like just one more hassle, but it adds shine and helps the colour last longer, too.

5 If you are right-handed, painting those nails will always be trickier. Keep practising. If the varnish goes everywhere, don't panic. Dip a cotton bud in varnish remover and use it to tidy up.

Step-by-step manicure

The long version. For when you've got a quiet night in, or a sleepover or just feel like indulging yourself.

YOU WILL NEED
Nail-varnish remover
Cotton wool
Nail scissors
Nail file
Cuticle cream
Bowl of warm water
Cuticle stick
Cuticle-clippers
Hand cream
Clear varnish for base coat and top coat
Nail varnish

1 & 2

3

1 Remove old nail varnish.

2 Trim nails, then file them into the shape you want.

3 Rub a bit of cuticle cream into the nail beds, then soak the fingers of whichever hand isn't being worked on in the bowl of warm water for a few minutes.

4 Using a bit of cotton wool wrapped around the tip of the cuticle stick, loosen the cuticles if they have been sticking to the nails, and push them back. Do it gently. It's tempting to push and prod at them but if you tear them, it will be sore. If there are long loose bits of cuticle, cut them off neatly with cuticle-clippers.

5 Massage hand cream into your hands.

6 Wipe over the nails with soapy water to get traces of hand cream/cuticle cream off nails.

7 Apply clear base coat to cover up any roughness in the nail and give a smooth surface to paint onto. This will also stop coloured varnish from staining your nails.

8 Paint on two coats of colour, avoiding painting over the cuticles at the base of the nail. Leave a few minutes between each coat. Finish with a layer of clear top coat.

The quick version

When you don't have the time for the full works...

✱ Remove old nail varnish.

✱ Cut nails and/or file them to neaten the edges and shape them.

✱ Repaint – and off you go.

4

How to make a manicure last

A nail-salon manicure can last the best part of a week. Here's how to make the home version hold up:

✱ Add a new layer of top coat each day, for protection.

✱ Wear rubber gloves for washing up.

✱ Refuse to help around the house!

THINGS THAT WRECK A MANICURE:

✱ Water. Don't soak your hands in the bath or the washing-up bowl.

✱ Bashing your nails on things.

✱ Using nails as tools.

5 & 6

7

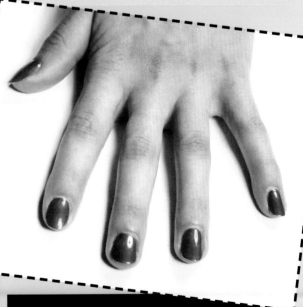

8

Tip

Try a quick-dry or one-coat varnish for a speedier finish.

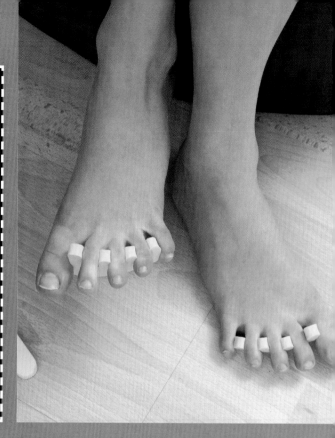

Step-by-step pedicure

YOU WILL NEED

Nail-varnish remover
Cotton wool
Nail-clippers
Nail file
Cuticle cream
Bowl of warm water
Foot scrub
Cuticle stick
Cuticle-clippers
Hand (or foot) cream
Toe separators, or two tissues
Clear varnish for base coat and topcoat
Nail varnish

1 Remove any old nail varnish.

2 Trim nails using the clippers and then file them smooth. Keep them shaped straight (if you file them down at the sides, they can more easily become ingrown).

3 Rub cuticle cream into the nail beds and then soak the feet in the bowl of warm water for a few minutes. Rub feet with foot scrub. Rinse well and dry.

4 Wrap a bit of cotton wool round the cuticle stick and ease cuticles back from the nails. As with fingernails, if there are lots of bits of stray cuticle, remove them with cuticle-clippers.

5 Massage hand cream into your feet.

6 Wipe over the nails with soapy water to remove traces of hand cream/cuticle cream from nails.

7 Put the toe separators in place, or fold a tissue lengthwise into a long ribbon and wind it in and out of the toes on each foot. It may not seem to move them far away from one another but it makes nails easier to paint and stops them smudging while they dry.

8 Paint on clear base coat. Paint on two coats of colour. Finish with a layer of clear top coat. Allow to dry!

The quick version

✱ Paint the nails using base coat, two coats of colour and top coat, but don't worry if it splashes all over the edges of the nails. Let the whole lot dry before you go to bed.

✱ In the morning, cover your toes with a thick layer of foot cream or balm.

✱ Have a bath and, using an old toothbrush, scrub gently at the edges of the nails where the varnish has splashed over. The extra bits of varnish will come off easily and your toes will look perfect.

How to do a great foot rub

You can do this for yourself if you're reasonably flexible, but it's much nicer to get someone else to do it for you (you might have to massage their feet first). If you have time, soak the feet in a basin of warm water before you start, perhaps with a drop of eucalyptus or citronella oil.

1 Start by stretching and flexing the feet, bending them forwards and backwards. Rotate them gently on the ankles, and twist the feet between your hands. (It's easier to do this bit before you start covering them in foot lotion or balm.)

2 Take a good handful of whatever you're going to rub the feet with. Body lotion, foot balm, thick body butter, hand cream, it doesn't matter. If the person who's being massaged can't stand slippery stuff on their feet, you could try using foot powder or talc, which is less gungy but still lets you slide your fingers over the skin more smoothly.

3 Start massaging whatever you've chosen into the feet with firm strong movements, going up over the top of feet, round the ankles and the back of the heels, and covering the soles of the feet, too. Ask if you've got the pressure right. You don't want the other person wincing with pain or creasing up because it's too ticklish.

Tip

Don't press too hard, unless you are asked to. Feet can be surprisingly sensitive, or have sensitive spots, and it's impossible to know what is nice for someone else unless they tell you.

4 Work down the top of the foot – do this with the foot pointing towards you, your thumbs on top of the foot and your fingers underneath. Run your thumbs down in between the bones on the foot, sweeping down towards the gaps between the toes. Don't press too hard.

5 Massage up and down the underside of the foot. You can use your thumbs to work into the ball of the foot, using little circular movements, or you can make your knuckles into a fist and carefully work that across the ball of the foot and then down the middle of the foot (watch out, this is likely to be a tickly spot).

6 Massage the toes, one by one, pulling gently from where they join the foot down to the tips. Repeat the steps with the other foot, then finish by wiping the feet with a towel so that they're not slippery. Finally, hold both feet gently in your hands for a few seconds to bring the foot rub to an end.

Green nails!

Can you have cool nail colours and be eco-friendly too?

Q Nail varnish smells great. Is that because it's full of chemicals?

Yes, it's full of chemicals, but you use it in such small quantities that these are not harmful.

Q Why are some nail varnishes called "toluene-free"? What is toluene and is it dangerous?

Toluene is a chemical used to make nail varnish look smooth and stick evenly onto your nails – it does a great job but it can be toxic if you breathe in too much of it, which is why you should always use nail varnish in a well-ventilated room. Painting your own nails in your own bedroom isn't going to poison you; it's more of a problem for manicurists who use varnish all day in a cramped room.

Q What about acetone? Lots of nail-varnish removers are "acetone-free" – is acetone bad too?

It's not dangerous but it does dry out the nails, so an acetone-free varnish remover is better.

Q How do I know if a varnish has toluene in it?

It appears on ingredients lists as toluene, benzene, toluol or methylbenzene.

Q Is there such a thing as "green" nail varnish?

No. It's pretty toxic stuff, what with the toluene and another chemical, formaldehyde, which

has been shown to cause cancer in animals. New nail varnishes are being developed that are water-based, so don't need the powerful chemical solvents normally used in nail varnish; when those become more widely available, they will be the greener option. The other green option is to keep your nails natural, and make them shine with a nail-buffer rather than polish.

Teeth

Brushing my teeth has just got to be done, and I know a quick once-over morning and evening isn't good enough. Still, it always seems like the biggest chore and words like "floss" and "plaque" aren't anything to get excited about. But I don't want to end up with rotting teeth like the pictures I've seen at the dentist's. So it's back to the sink. If I play music at the same time, two minutes go by much more quickly.

Keeping teeth clean

How well you brush makes a big difference to the end result.

1. Brush. Start with the brush at a 45-degree angle to the gums (with the bristles tilted against the gums, rather than at a right angle to them).

2. Move the brush in small circles, rather than scrubbing against the teeth.

3. Work around the outside of your upper teeth, then the inside.

4. Repeat with the lower teeth.

5. Brush the flat, biting surfaces of your back teeth.

6. Brush your tongue.

7. Floss.

8. Rinse with mouthwash.

Q Do I really have to brush my teeth twice a day?

Yes, you really, really do. It keeps your teeth healthy, gets rid of plaque and freshens your breath, too. It will also save you a lot of costly dentist bills when you're older.

DID YOU KNOW?

BRUSHING YOUR TEETH BEFORE BREAKFAST IS AS GOOD AS BRUSHING THEM AFTERWARDS. JUST MAKE SURE THAT THE OTHER TIME YOU BRUSH THEM IS LAST THING AT NIGHT.

Q Are electric toothbrushes better than ordinary brushes?

Yes. They are more efficient and they do a better job than normal brushes.

Q How long do I have to brush my teeth for? I can get them clean in 30 seconds.

Thirty seconds is just a quick whisk round. It won't get out all the old bits of food, let alone remove the plaque. To clean them properly you need to brush for two whole minutes.

Q Why do I have to go to the dentist twice a year when there's nothing wrong with my teeth?

Just to check. If anything is starting to go wrong, the dentist will spot it before it turns into a major problem.

Q Are expensive toothpastes better than cheap ones?

No. As long as the toothpaste you use has fluoride in it, it doesn't make much difference which you use.

Q What is fluoride?

It's a mineral which helps strengthen your teeth against attack from bacteria.

Q Are any of the chemicals in toothpaste bad for you?

None of them are "bad". Some people prefer to avoid sodium lauryl sulphate (SLS), which is what makes toothpaste foam up. It can irritate the mouth, but only if you are unusually sensitive to it.

Q What can I use instead of toothpaste containing SLS?

You can try a natural toothpaste that doesn't contain SLS, but your dentist would be happier if you used a fluoride mouthwash with it. Most natural toothpastes don't contain fluoride, and without fluoride, you're asking for tooth decay to set in.

Q Do I need to use mouthwash as well as doing all of this?

You don't have to, but it helps. Mouthwash keeps down the number of bacteria in your mouth and keeps your breath fresher for longer. It also gives teeth a dose of fluoride.

Brush first or floss first?

Even dentists argue about this. But they agree you should floss at least once every day.

How to floss your teeth

1. Pull off a length of floss (25–30 cm).
2. Wrap one end around the middle finger of each hand (then your index fingers are free to move the floss into place).
3. Using your thumbs and forefingers, slide the floss between two teeth.
4. Curl the floss around the tooth, keeping it taut, and work it up (or down) to the gums and back.
5. Curl it around the tooth from the other side and clean that bit.
6. Move the floss along past one tooth, and carry on.
7. If you have trouble, ask one of the staff to demonstrate next time you go to the dentist.

Plaque & decay

These are your teeth's main enemies. Here's how to beat 'em.

Q What is plaque and why is it so bad?

It's an invisible sticky film that forms on the surface of teeth. If you don't make an effort to clean plaque off your teeth really well, it will cause tooth decay. It can also build up and harden into a yellowish cement called tartar, and can increase your chances of getting gum disease.

Q How do I deal with plaque?

Brush properly, then use dental floss to get at the bits your brush can't reach. And try to eat less sugary stuff.

Q What does sugar have to do with plaque?

As soon as you eat anything sugary, the bacteria in plaque make your saliva more acidic. This acid attacks the enamel that covers your teeth. The result is tooth decay.

Q Does that mean I shouldn't ever eat sweets?

In an ideal world, yes! But in real life? Sucking on mints, chewing gummy sweets or slowly sipping your way through a large, sugary fizzy drink are the worst things for your teeth because they cover them repeatedly in sugar, which sets off the bacteria ... so when you eat something sweet, try to brush your teeth as soon as you can afterwards. If you know you're about to have a sweet-fest, there are two ways to limit the damage. Before you start scoffing, rinse your mouth with fluoride mouthwash, or swish your mouth with milk. This will act as a coating and put a bit of calcium on the teeth which helps neutralize the acid. You could also chew sugar-free gum (choose one with xylitol).

Q Is brushing the only way to stop this going on?

There are other ways to get your saliva back to normal. Eating an alkaline food such as cheese or drinking some milk will lower the level of acid in your saliva, as will chewing gum. But none of these removes plaque, so you still need to brush.

DID YOU KNOW?

GETTING RID OF PLAQUE HELPS TO KEEP YOUR HEART HEALTHY AS WELL AS YOUR TEETH. THERE IS A STRONG LINK BETWEEN GUM DISEASE AND CLOGGED ARTERIES IN THE HEART.

Q **What about eating an apple?**
Actually, that will make it worse. Apples are healthy things to eat, but they contain a lot of sugar. So they will make your saliva acidic, too.

How to see where plaque is hiding

YOU WILL NEED
A bottle of food colouring

1. Dab a cotton bud in colouring and rub it round your teeth and gums (scary, if you use blue).
2. Rinse, then take a look to see where the plaque is clinging on.

If you don't fancy the food-colouring option, you can get some disclosing tablets from the chemist instead.

When your toothbrush starts to look a bit frayed it's time to get a new one. Worn-out brushes don't clean your teeth properly.

Staining & whitening

Good tooth hygiene will keep teeth white as well as healthy.

Q My teeth never look very white...

Normal teeth are a lightish yellow – no teeth are naturally dazzlingly white. The way to keep yours as white as possible is to brush properly twice a day. Most of the stains that end up on teeth are because of bad habits like eating lots of sugary things and not brushing properly – and tea and coffee, too.

Q Do whitening toothpastes work?

Yes, at least they help you to brush off any stains that are trying to settle onto your teeth,

but they won't make your teeth any whiter than nature intended. Watch out for scratchy ones, which can damage the enamel on the tooth's surface.

Q Can I use baking soda to get teeth whiter?

Absolutely totally NO WAY! Scrubbing soda onto teeth will damage the enamel.

Q What about teeth-bleaching kits off the internet?

Don't risk it. Many of them will contain ingredients that could damage your teeth.

Q Is there anything else I can do without cosmetic whitening?

Ask your dentist to scale and polish your teeth instead, which is a less aggressive way to get them clean and gleaming.

DID YOU KNOW?

IF YOU DRINK DARK-COLOURED FIZZY DRINKS THROUGH A STRAW, THEY WILL STAIN YOUR TEETH LESS. (BUT THEY'RE STILL NOT GOOD FOR YOU.)

THINGS THAT STAIN YOUR TEETH

Curry   dark-coloured fizzy drinks   **Cigarettes**

COFFEE   **TEA**   *Some antibiotics*

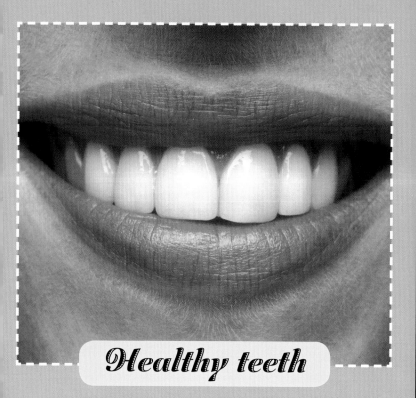

Healthy teeth

Six ways to avoid bad breath

✻ Brush your teeth regularly
✻ Use an (alcohol-free) mouthwash
✻ Chew parsley (it's what they used to do in the olden days, because it works!)
✻ Chew sugar-free gum
✻ Drink plenty of water
✻ Scrape or brush your tongue

Expert tips

From leading cosmetic dentist Dr Uchenna Okoye, founder of the London Smiling practices

- - - - - - - - - - - - - - - -

✻ Teeth are something you have to look after. Put in the preventative work now and you won't end up with the damage later.

✻ Fluoride toothpaste is the only thing that strengthens your teeth against attack from bacteria. It's like washing every day: you need to keep doing it. Your dentist can get you a high-fluoride toothpaste for extra help.

✻ Floss, regularly. Most cavities form between the teeth, where plaque has been left to attack teeth.

✻ Get an electric toothbrush. They do a better job and usually have a built-in timer.

✻ If there is any hint that you need to wear braces, wear them. Most of my adult patients complain that their parents should have made them wear braces.

✻ Don't even think about cosmetic dental whitening treatments before you are 18. Your teeth are still developing.

✻ Choose alcohol-free mouthwash. No, it won't make you drunk, but alcohol has been linked to mouth cancer. Play safe and avoid it.

I know that what I eat affects my health, skin, mood, brain power and energy levels, so it's essential to eat all the right stuff to stay sane and healthy. Wholegrain carbs, protein, masses of fruit and veg, oily fish, good fats ... they're all vital but life's too

Eating well

short to spend feeling guilty over the odd doughnut. Food is something to be enjoyed – particularly with your friends and family. And a few squares of chocolate never hurt anyone.

How to do it

What should you eat and what should you avoid? Here's the low-down.

Q Where do I start?

Eating well is largely common sense, backed up by good habits (you know deep down that it's better to snack on carrots than on crisps). It doesn't mean expensive ingredients or difficult recipes, just sensible decisions.

Q So what's the best way to go about it?

Make it your mission to eat the good stuff first, to pack in the nutrients, and save the treats (sweets, junk food, fizzy drinks) for occasional indulgence. You do need a touch of self-discipline, but eating right shouldn't feel like a sacrifice. Food is something to be enjoyed, not something to be afraid of.

Q Why are you so keen that I eat protein all the time?

It helps you to feel full and slows down the rate at which your body digests carbohydrates, so it helps to balance your blood sugar levels. You don't have to eat red meat or fish. Nuts and seeds are full of protein. So are cottage cheese and beans.

Q You always tell me not to eat sugar. Why is sugar so bad?

Eating sugar plays havoc with your blood sugar levels and, if you do it too often, your body can become deaf to its own demands for insulin (see below). That's called "insulin resistance", which in turn can lead to diabetes.

Q What do you mean by "blood sugar levels" exactly?

These are a measure of how much glucose there is in your blood. All the starchy and sugary carbohydrates that you eat get broken down into glucose molecules, which travel round your body in the bloodstream and are used as fuel for your brain and your muscles. When you eat wholegrain or "complex" carbs (brown rice, wholemeal bread, fruit and vegetables), they take a while to digest, giving your body a good, steady supply of energy. But when you eat sugary foods or refined carbs (sweets, white bread, white pasta), these are broken down really quickly and you get a surge of glucose in the blood – a sugar "high" – and you may feel all buzzy and giggly. Your pancreas then has to produce insulin quickly to deal with this sudden rush of sugar (which it does by storing the extra glucose as fat), and when it has done that, your blood sugar levels may be a bit lower than ideal, which leaves you feeling cross, tired and craving sweet things.

Q And is fat bad for me, too?

Fat isn't such a baddie. Yes, foods that are high in fat are high in calories, which means they can be fattening, but every cell in your body needs the right kind of fat in order to function properly.

Q What's the right kind of fat?

Unsaturated fats (particularly omega-3 essential fatty acids, i.e. the kind that you find in oily fish, seeds and some nuts). Not butter or the fat you get in fatty meat (saturated fats) or the fat that comes in chocolate or deep-fried foods.

Tip

Learn to listen to your body and what it's asking for (unless it's crying out for doughnuts). And when you've had enough, stop eating. There's no law that says you have to clear your plate.

EATING WELL

RECIPES FROM SAM STERN'S
REAL FOOD REAL FAST

WALKER BOOKS £9.99

Speedy food to go

When I'm in a hurry and need to grab something to eat, I'd rather not reach for junk food. There are some of my favourite speedy snacks from teenage cook, Sam Stern.

BREAKFAST BOOST SMOOTHIE
YOU WILL NEED
A banana ✱ handful blueberries ✱ handful raspberries ✱ ½ pint milk ✱ drizzle of honey
METHOD
1. Wash the soft fruit (use frozen fruit if you can't get fresh).
2. Peel the banana. Break it into bits with your fingers and chuck it in the jug of your blender.
3. Drop in the soft fruit.
4. Drizzle in the honey.
5. Pour in milk to cover fruit. Sub in a bit of plain yogurt if you like.
6. Blitz it. Drink it.

BERRY YOGURT CRUNCH
YOU WILL NEED
A handful of berries of choice ✱ runny honey ✱ 150 ml/5 fl oz pot of natural, vanilla or honey yogurt ✱ 2 tbsps crunchy cereal
METHOD
1. Chuck washed berries into a bowl.
2. Mix yogurt, a drizzle of honey and cereal in another.
3. Tip over berries. Top with more cereal.

HUMMUS & VEG PLATE
YOU WILL NEED
Hummus ✱ carrots ✱ celery ✱ cucumber ✱ courgettes ✱ red peppers ✱ yellow peppers
METHOD
1. Slap hummus into a bowl. Sit bowl on larger plate.
2. Peel and slice carrots and celery lengthways. Wash and slice courgettes and cucumber lengthways. Halve your peppers. Cut out seeds and joinery. Slice.
3. Arrange veg round hummus.

TOMATO AND GARLIC TOAST
YOU WILL NEED
2 slices bread ✱ extra virgin olive oil ✱ 1 clove garlic ✱ 1 ripe tomato
METHOD
1. Make toast. Slap on plate.
2. Drizzle each toast with a little olive oil.
3. Cut garlic clove in half. Rub over toast.
4. Cut tomato in half. Rub and squeeze half a tomato over each toast.
5. Chuck away used tomato. Enjoy.

Q Can't I just take vitamin pills and fish oils to make sure I get enough nutrients?

A fish-oil or omega-3 supplement is a great idea, because almost no one eats enough essential fatty acids. But for reasons scientists haven't yet worked out, the body doesn't treat vitamin pills in the same way that it treats vitamins and minerals found in food. So it's better to eat a varied diet with plenty of fruit and veg – then you shouldn't need vitamin pills.

Q And what will all this do for my skin? You said before that what I eat makes no difference to my skin.

What you eat has no effect on whether your skin is spotty or not. Eating well and getting all the nutrients your body needs can make an enormous difference to your general health and that shows up in your skin.

Q This all sounds great, but it's not easy when everyone else is eating giant choc-chip cookies at break-time.

You don't have to be perfect all the time. Follow the "80:20" rule, which means that if you are making good choices and eating the right stuff 80 per cent of the time, you can eat whatever you want for the other 20 per cent of the time. Remember that there is only so much you can do about your size and shape. Is your mother pear-shaped, or straight up and down? You can blame her if you are the same.

Q What about dieting?

Your friends are bound to talk about diets, but bear in mind that dieting is a fool's game and one that you rarely win. Forget counting calories, too. It makes you think you can swap, say, salmon and vegetables for a chocolate bar. Nutritionally, there's no contest. Learn to eat well and you'll feel great, you'll look good and you won't need to resort to dieting. And your body will thank you for it.

If you find it hard to pack down enough fruit and vegetables, think creatively. Fruit juice counts as a portion of fruit.

Expert tips

From Kate Cook, nutrition coach.

✱ The easiest way to keep your blood sugar levels steady and give yourself a steady supply of energy is to choose foods that are:
   Dense (heavy)
   Fibrous (like veg, fruit or wholegrain foods)
   High in protein
and AVOID foods that are:
   Sweet
   Fluffy (light in weight like puffed-rice cereals, or fluffy like mashed potatoes)
   White (like white bread or white pasta)

✱ Always eat a good breakfast. Eggs or muesli is a good idea because foods like this fill you up, keep your energy balanced and stop you reaching for the junky snacks mid-morning.

✱ Fizzy drinks and diet fizzy drinks are no good for you and do not satisfy thirst. When your energy levels are low and you want a caffeinated drink as a pick-me-up, try drinking a glass of water and eating something to boost your blood sugar levels instead.

✱ Drink enough water. Carry a bottle with you so you aren't left high and dry. Staying hydrated helps your concentration as well as your health.

✱ Don't be tempted by fad diets. They may work in the short term but they make you put on weight in the long run and then you end up in a yo-yo pattern of never-ending dieting. Get on with being who you are and not looking round at celebs and what they're eating (or not). They often have a lot of money and no sense!

Fragrance

Perfume seems to me to be like an invisible but really useful type of make-up. Wearing it makes me feel more confident – and it's always good to know you smell nice. But how come one scent can smell different on different people when it's the same stuff? Choosing a perfume ought to be really easy, since there are so many of them, but how do you find that special one that's right for you? I don't know where to start.

Choosing perfume

The right fragrance can be your "signature". Yours is out there waiting for you to find it.

Q Where do I start?
Try every kind of fragrance that you can get your hands on, from the ones your friends are wearing to your mum's favourites – and every time you go to a chemist or department store where there are testers, give them a whirl. It may not sound very scientific but that way, you can start to work out which ones appeal most to you.

Q Why do some scents smell great at first, but then really foul a bit later?
Most fragrances have three "notes" – a top note, a middle note and a base note, a bit like musical notes that go together to form a chord. The first "hit" of a perfume that you smell includes lots of the top notes, which are tiny molecules that evaporate quite quickly. After five minutes, you will be smelling the middle notes, and after half an hour, the base notes. You need to know that you like what is left at the end before you commit to buying.

Q Some perfumes smell amazing on my friends but they don't smell the same on me. Why?
Lots of factors affect how your skin smells – from your body chemistry and your diet to how oily your skin is. And the smell of your skin in turn can affect how the perfume will smell on you.

Q Why are some perfumes so expensive?
A perfume's price depends on many things – how pure and rare the ingredients are, whether it is made in small batches or mass produced, and how concentrated the fragrance is. A plain Parfum (pure perfume) will cost more than an Eau de Parfum, which will cost more than an Eau de Toilette.

Q I feel I don't know enough to make the right choice.
The great thing with perfume is that there is no right or wrong. Some people might have you think there was, but it's a bit like Art (with a capital A). Whether you prefer modern art, cartoons or Old Masters doesn't make you a better or worse person. It's the same with perfume. Just choose what you like, and don't worry about it.

Tip
Fragrance smells stronger and lasts better on moist skin.

How to try perfumes

✳ Spray a little into the inside of the lid of the bottle and sniff that. (Then if you hate it, you aren't stuck with it on your skin.)

✳ If you're in a shop and they have special perfume-testing spills of paper, spray each fragrance that you like onto a separate one and take all your favourites away to think about.

✳ If you find one or two you really like, spray a tiny bit of each onto your skin. Leave them for an hour before deciding that you can't live without them.

✳ Don't try too many at once. Your nose will get confused.

FRAGRANCE

Types of perfume

Type of fragrance	Smells	Classic examples	Modern examples	Personality
FLORAL	Flowery, sweet, heady	Joy (Jean Patou) No 5 (Chanel) Beautiful (Estée Lauder)	Tommy Girl (Tommy Hilfiger) Flower (Kenzo) Daisy (Marc Jacobs) Miss Dior Chérie (Dior)	Cute, girly, happy, easy-going
ORIENTAL	Spicy and exotic	Shalimar (Guerlain) Youth Dew (Estée Lauder) Dune (Dior)	Angel (Thierry Mugler) Just Cavalli Her (Roberto Cavalli)	Mysterious, seductive, unpredictable
CHYPRE (pronounced *sheep-ruh*)	Mossy, woody, fresh, sweet or bitter	Ma Griffe (Carven) Mitsouko (Guerlain)	Aromatics Elixir (Clinique) Agent Provocateur Strip (Agent Provocateur)	Sweet but can be surprisingly moody
CITRUS	Zesty, fresh, deliciously sharp, like lemons and oranges	Eau de Guerlain (Guerlain) Eau d'Hadrien (Annick Goutal)	Lime, Basil & Mandarin Cologne (Jo Malone) ck one (Calvin Klein)	Bright, effervescent, cheerful and straightforward
WOODY	Resiny, woody scents, often masculine	Vetiver (Guerlain) Magie Noire (Lancôme)	Palazzo (Fendi) En Sens de Bois (Miller Harris)	Original, doesn't follow the crowd and doesn't mind being different
COLOGNE	Wake-you-up fresh, zingy	Eau d'Orange Verte (Hermès) 4711 cologne	French Connection Fragrance (FCUK) Purple Water (Asprey)	Practical, sporty, doesn't hang around for long

Grab a few friends, line up the nail varnish, dig out some face masks or whip up your own, then get ready to spa. A bit of pampering is always a

Fun fun fun

treat, even if it's just relaxing in the bath. And it doesn't have to cost the earth either. It makes me feel better and de-stresses me. Everyone needs a bit of me-time to help them feel gorgeous and radiant.

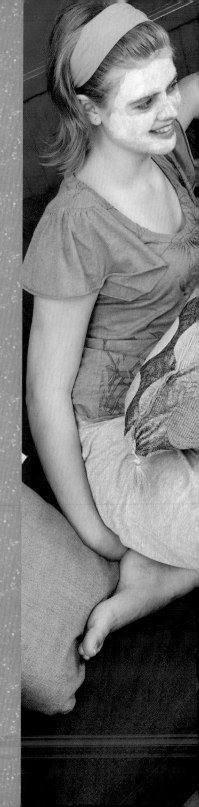

How to host a pamper party

Invite your friends
Decide on treatments
Prepare the food and drinks
Create a relaxing party atmosphere

1. Invite your friends

Ask them to bring comfortable clothes for relaxing in (preferably ones that won't be ruined if they get a bit of face mask on them) and flip-flops, so that if they have a pedicure, their toenails can dry.

2. Decide on treatments

Draw up a list of treatments – and what you'll need for them. You don't need everything on this list, it's just to give you ideas. If you don't have some of the things you want to use, see what your friends could bring. Take it in turns to work on one another.

Manicures and pedicures

You will need: aromatherapy oil, bowls of warm water, nail files, nail-clippers, nail scissors. Cotton wool and nail varnish remover, cotton buds, clear nail varnish for base coat and top coat, coloured nail varnish, a few small towels.

Make it look professional by creating a "nail station" at the end of the kitchen table, or at a small table (it's much easier to do someone's nails if they are sitting opposite you). Lay out a towel for them to rest their hands on, and on your side, lay out a folded flannel with your tools and bottles in a neat row on it.

How to do it: see page 114.

Foot massage

You will need: a basin of warm water with a drop of aromatherapy oil in it (eucalyptus or tea-tree is cleansing and antiseptic), foot scrub, foot balm or lotion for massage.

How to do it: soak feet in warm water for a couple of minutes. Rub them all over with the foot scrub and rinse them clean. Do the foot massage sitting opposite the person you are working on, so that you can rest their foot in your lap while you work on it. Follow the instructions on page 119.

Tip: do this before a pedicure, or work it in as part of the pedicure routine.

Mini facial

You will need: cleansing lotion, bowl of hot water, flannel, face mask (and sponge or cotton wool for removing this), moisturizer. See page 41 for technique.

Face masks
Find a tube of your favourite or try the recipes on page 38.

Hairdressing
You will need: styling sprays or lotions, hairdryer, a variety of hair brushes and a tail-comb, curling tongs and/or straighteners and/or crimpers, hair texturizer or hairspray.

3. Prepare the food and drinks

Drinks

Smoothies

For each smoothie, you will need
2 portions of soft, blendable fruit (e.g.
a handful strawberries or blueberries, a
medium banana, a small chopped pear,
half a mango)
250 ml milk
1 tbsp plain yogurt
Ice cubes
Blend them to your guests' requests!

Mocktails

These non-alcoholic cocktails taste delicious.
For a professional finish, dip the rims of the
glasses in egg white, then into a saucer of
sugar. Decorate with fancy stirrers or paper
parasols.

Pina colada

50 ml coconut cream
150 ml pineapple juice
Shake or stir the ingredients together, then
pour them into a glass containing two ice
cubes.

Shirley Temple

100 ml ginger ale
50 ml orange juice
1 tsp grenadine syrup

Shake together and pour over crushed ice
(ice cubes whizzed up in the blender or food
processor). Garnish with a maraschino cherry
and a thin slice of orange.

Cola float

Put 1 large scoop of vanilla ice cream in the
bottom of a large glass, then fill up the glass
with cola and stir carefully (this one is best
without ice).

Food

Nachos

A couple of packets of tortilla chips
A jar of tomato salsa
A tub of guacamole
A bowl of soured cream
A tin of refried beans
2 balls mozzarella
100 g strong Cheddar cheese, grated

Put a layer of tortilla chips on a baking tray,
spread a layer of refried beans over them,
scatter with chopped mozzarella and grated
Cheddar. Repeat the layering, ending with
cheese on top. Put in a hot oven for 20
minutes until everything is hot through and the
cheese is gooey and melted, then serve with
all your extras.

Fruit kebabs

Chop fruit into chunks and thread the chunks
on wooden skewers. Make them colourful

with red and green grapes, strawberries, pineapple...

Bear in mind that apple and pear will go brown unless you dip the cut pieces in a bowl of water to which you have added a few drops of lemon juice.

Chocolate fondue

Melt a big bar or two of chocolate by breaking it into chunks and putting these in a bowl that you can rest in a pan of hot water (don't put the chocolate directly into the saucepan; it sounds as though it should work, and faster, but it just goes into strange lumps). Stir slowly as it melts. Then dip fruit or marshmallows into the melted chocolate and enjoy.

4. *Create a relaxing party atmosphere*

✱ Use small lamps for soft lighting.

✱ Arrange little candles or tealights into groups.

✱ Burn a stick of incense

or a scented candle to perfume the air.

✱ Float flowers in a bowl of water for an eastern spa touch.

✱ Choose your music: line up your top CDs or make a playlist of your favourite songs.

Discover aromatherapy

Aromatherapy sounds wonderful, but what's it for and how do I get started?

Q What is aromatherapy?
It's a way of using gorgeous-smelling essential oils which have been extracted from plants and flowers to enhance your life and your health.

Q How does it work?
The tiny volatile molecules that give essential oils their smell appear to have a mood-boosting, feel-good effect on your mind and spirits and a physical effect on the body, too.

Q "Appear to have"? Then is it for real or not?
Plenty of studies have shown that essential oils such as tea-tree have anti-bacterial properties, and that inhaling lavender essence can slow down your reaction times (which is why it's good for relaxation, but not one to use at school). Aromatherapy can have a huge effect on your emotional well-being, but there is no scientific evidence to show that it will directly benefit your health. So that's yes and no.

Q How do you know which oils to use?
Follow your nose (and see the chart below). Try as many oils and oil blends as you can and see which you like and which make you feel good.

Choosing the right oil

Lavender	"Cooling" and relaxing and good for calming the nervous system.
Rosemary & juniper	"Warming", which makes them good for relaxing muscles after you have played sport or been for a long walk. These two oils make the mind feel more alert, too.
Tea-tree, pine, eucalyptus, ravensara	All good for helping you to breathe more easily. You could use them before exercise, or when you are feeling stuffy with a cold.
Patchouli	Earthy and antiseptic, often used in perfume.
Jasmine, ylang ylang	These two are both sweet and delicate, with an intoxicating smell that you'll recognize in many perfumes.
Lemongrass	Smells fresh and zesty. Don't use it on the skin without diluting it.

Expert tips

Essential oils are strong and should be used with care. Follow these tips from Danièle Ryman, a leading aromatherapist.

✳ Essential oils are strong and need to be mixed into a base oil, to dilute them, before you use them for massage, or for bath oils, or as ultra-natural perfumes. Good base oils for dry skin include: almond, jojoba, argan and borage oil (which is full of omega-3 fatty acids, making it particularly good for the skin). If your skin is oily, use a lighter oil like grapeseed or soya oil as a base.

✳ Don't use too much. It's tempting to think that if one drop is good, then four will be better, but aromatherapy doesn't work like that. Using too much is a waste of the oils and may make you feel a bit peculiar. Essential oils are not like modern perfumes, with a smell that will be strong for hours and hours. As the molecules evaporate from the oil, the smell will disappear.

✳ Choose essential oils carefully. If an oil seems surprisingly cheap, it is probably because it has been diluted. Some, like rose or neroli (orange blossom), which are difficult to produce, can be very expensive. If they're too expensive to buy with your allowance, try asking for a selection of oils as a present.

✳ If you pop a few drops of wheatgerm oil into a mixture that you have made, it will add vitamin E, which is very good for the skin, and will also help to stop the oil going rancid so quickly.

Using essential oils at home

In the bath

Run your bath first, then add a drop or two of essential oil just before you get in, so that you get the benefit of the fragrant oils. Use lavender oil to help you relax.

To help you concentrate

To wake up your mind, try peppermint, rosemary or geranium oil. Rub one drop between your hands and inhale the fumes for a few seconds.

To clear a stuffy nose & sinuses

Put a drop of eucalyptus oil into a bowl of hot water, then lower your face over the bowl. Cover your head (and the bowl) with a towel and inhale the soothing vapour.

To make your room smell great

You can use an oil burner (though aromatherapists complain that these can burn the oil) or, even easier, put a drop of oil into a small bowl of hot water and let

the fragrant molecules diffuse around the room. Try lemongrass oil, which smells clean and uplifting.

To tackle spots
Tea-tree oil is a great antiseptic. Using a cotton bud, dab it onto spots to help soothe inflammation.

To soothe burns
Dab the burned skin with undiluted lavender oil. It is particularly good at helping scorched skin heal faster than usual.

As a massage oil
Add a few drops of your favourite oil to a base oil, then massage into your limbs.

DANIÈLE RYMAN'S SOOTHING BEDTIME MASSAGE OIL
1 tbsp almond oil
1 drop essential oil of melissa
2 drops essential oil of frankincense
1 drop essential oil of basil
2 drops essential oil of lavender, orange, petit grain or neroli

Mix the oils together. Starting at your feet, massage the oil gently into your skin. Work up your legs, the bits of your back that you can reach, your neck and chest, using long, slow movements and breathing slowly and deeply, to make the most of the wonderful smell of the oils. Then lie down, relax and drift off to sleep!

Time to relax
Bathtime

Pick a time when you're not going to be interrupted by the rest of your family barging in or shouting to use the bathroom.

YOU WILL NEED

* A couple of small candles

* Aromatherapy oil for the bath (or bubble bath if you must, but it's not so good for your skin)

* A neck pillow, so you can lean back on the end of the bath

* Something to tie your hair up with, or a shower cap to get it up out of the way

* Soothing music – preferably from a portable stereo that doesn't need plugging in. (If it's something with a plug, don't put it in a position from where it could fall into the water and electrocute you.)

* A warm towel to wrap yourself in afterwards

Run the bath nice and deep, but not too hot. Light the candles, relax and enjoy!

Treats for your eyes

If your eyes look a bit tired or puffy after a long day at school, try one of these eye treatments to get them back to normal.

* Put slices of cucumber (preferably from a cucumber that has been in the fridge) on your closed eyes and lie down for ten minutes. Potato slices do a good job too, because they contain an effective de-puffing ingredient, but they're not as soft or flexible as cucumber slices and you need to rinse the starch off them first, to make them less sticky.

* Put tea bags on your eyes. (You need to make tea with them first, and then let them cool down!) Camomile tea bags are even more soothing than normal breakfast tea bags.

* Get an ice cube and slide it, very gently, over the puffy bits of your eyes.

How to look good in pictures

I don't mind having my picture taken, but it's embarrassing when I try to do a nice smile, then look completely cheesy. No one wants to look stupid in pictures, so lock yourself in your room with a camera and try these tips.

1 If you don't know what to do with your hands, try putting them in your pockets, or find something to hold (a friend's arm, a pet, a handbag), sit on or lean against. Try not to fold your arms as that usually looks defensive, as if you're putting up a barrier between you and the camera.

2 Stand slightly sideways on to the camera, then turn to look back at the lens. It's much more flattering than if you stand head on to the camera.

3 Don't say cheese, say "brush". It lifts up all the contours of the face and makes you look happier.

4 Find a friend to pose with. That often makes it easier, and that's the one time when folding your arms looks fine – if you both stand back to back, fold your arms, then turn to smile at the camera.

5 If your face starts feeling really stiff and awkward and you know your smile will look fake, puff up your cheeks and roll your eyes (not while the camera is snapping!), then let it all go back to normal and the tension should be gone.

Expert tips

From leading portrait photographer, Chris Dawes.

✴ Look in the mirror and smile. Does it work? Does it look normal and natural and happy? If not, try to find a way of giving the impression of being happy and confident without smiling. Practise in front of a mirror.

✴ Learn to "project". That means putting your personality across to the camera. Look through the lens at the person behind it, and think about communicating with them.

✴ Your eyes can always say much more than just a smile. If you're going to smile, do it with your eyes as well as your mouth. If you put on a grin but are still looking daggers at the camera, it will show!

✴ Avoid having photographs taken at strange angles. Face the camera directly or with a slight shift to one side or the other. That way, you will be presenting the face that you see in the mirror (albeit reversed).

✴ Avoid overhead light, which can give you horrible shadows under the eyes and nose. And don't stick a torch under your chin unless you want to look like something from a horror movie.

INDEX

Acknowledgements

Molly and Alice would like to thank:

The brilliant team at Walker Books: Denise Johnstone-Burt, who calmly and patiently steered this book into being, Louise Jackson, who has made it look so fresh and appealing, and Ellen Holgate for all her hard work and good humour;

Suki Dhanda for her gorgeous photographs, www.sukidhanda.com;

Louise Constad for her steady hands and skilful make-up, and Emilie Yong (and Mini), www.beautyqueenworkshops.com;

Vanessa Chaudy for a perfect manicure;

Beth, Eliza, Emmie, Alex, Cat, Suki, Ifeoma, Rose, Nikki and Helena for being such great models and for letting us cover them with mashed avocado, body lotion, eyeliner and hair colouring;

Matthew and Robert for putting up with the household being even more over-run with make-up and girliness than usual;

Chris Smith, without whose encouragement none of the actual writing would have got done;

Selfridges, for allowing the girls to giggle their way around the beauty hall, closely pursued by a camera;

And of course to our agent, the delightful Simon Trewin.

Huge thanks too to the specialists who gave us their time and expertise:

Susan Baldwin, head of colour, John Frieda, London, 020 7491 0840;

Dr Susan Mayou, consultant dermatologist, Cadogan Clinic, London, www.cadoganclinic.com;

Charlotte Vøhtz, founder of The Green People Company, www.greenpeople.co.uk;

Jessica Hoffman, celebrity nail technician, John Frieda, London, 020 7491 0840;

Josephine Fairley and Sarah Stacey, founders of www.beautybible.com;

Dr Uchenna Okoye, aesthetic dentist, www.londonsmiling.com;

Kate Cook, nutritional therapist and life coach, www.thenutritioncoach.co.uk;

Danièle Ryman, aromatherapist, www.danieleryman.com;

Chris Dawes, portrait photographer, www.chrisdawes.com.

Disclaimer

First published 2009 by Walker Books Ltd
87 Vauxhall Walk, London SE11 5HJ

10 9 8 7 6 5 4

Text © 2009 Alice Hart-Davis and Molly Hindhaugh
Photographs © 2009 Walker Books Ltd
Photographs by Suki Dhanda
Illustrations © 2009 Debbie Powell

The right of Alice Hart-Davis and Molly Hindhaugh to be identified as authors of this work has been asserted by them in accordance with the Copyright, Designs and Patents Act 1988

This book has been typeset in Futura

Printed in China

British Library Cataloguing in Publication Data:
a catalogue record for this book is available from the British Library

ISBN 978-1-4063-1831-9

www.walker.co.uk